RECORDS OF THE PAST

BEING ENGLISH TRANSLATIONS

OF THE

ANCIENT MONUMENTS OF EGYPT AND

WESTERN ASIA

NEW SERIES

EDITED BY A. H. SAYCE
Hon. LL.D. Dublin; Hon. D.D. Edinburgh

VOL. IV

ISBN: 978-1-63923-914-6

All Rights reserved. No part of this book maybe reproduced without written permission from the publishers, except by a reviewer who may quote brief passages in a review to be printed in a newspaper or magazine.

Printed: March 2023

Published and Distributed By:
Lushena Books
607 Country Club Drive, Unit E
Bensenville, IL 60106
www.lushenabks.com

ISBN: 978-1-63923-914-6

THE GREAT INSCRIPTION OF AMEN-EM-HEB.[1]

1. As for me, I was the very faithful [2] [instrument] of the sovereign; the half of the heart of the king of the south, the light of the heart of the king of the north, while I followed
2. my master in his expeditions to the regions of the north or of the south, [those which] he desired; for I was as the companion of his feet, and that
3. in the midst of his valour and his power, in order to give testimony. Now I captured in the country of
4. NEKEB,[3] and brought back (certain) Asiatics, three

---

[1] The text of this great inscription has been published by Ebers in the Z. D. M. G., 1873, and in the *Mélanges* of Chabas (3d series). Stern (in the Z. D. M. G.) has proposed some corrections. A new edition of the text will appear in the *Mémoires* of the French mission at Cairo.

[2] *Mâ ur n ati ânkh uza senb* ("the true great one of the sovereign, who is life, power, and health," that is, "one who does things truly great," "who accomplishes the designs of his master.") The idea of confidence contained in that of truth may also indicate that the king had confidence in the fidelity of his servant.

[3] Here begin the campaigns of Amen-em-heb. It was in the 29th year of Thothmes III, since line 4 informs us that it happened when the king reached Naharain, and the following campaign (line 13) was directed against Kadesh, which was captured for the first time in the thirtieth year of Thothmes. Amen-em-heb therefore took no part in the battle of Megiddo in the twenty-third year, at which time he was doubtless still very young. Moreover, he did not enter the royal guard at once; he had first to traverse a considerable distance before he could present to the king, who was in Naharain, the prisoners he had taken in Nekeb. Nekeb is the Negeb or "southern country" of Palestine, frequently mentioned in the Old Testament (see Gen. xiii. 1, xx. 1; Josh. x. 40, etc.). The course of events would have been:—The federated Asiatics under the prince of Kadesh, taught by their recent defeats, seem to have avoided a battle, and fortified themselves in their cities, which had to be besieged one after the other. Hence Thothmes, with the main part of his army, occupied himself with this work, while flying columns compelled the chiefs who would

PREFACE

THANKS to my contributors, I have this year been able to redeem my promise of issuing two volumes of the *Records of the Past* during the same season. The monumental records of the ancient oriental world are so numerous, and so much new material is continually being brought to light, that it is difficult for either contributors or editors to keep pace with the discoveries that are constantly being made. All we can hope to do is to lay before the public the most important of the documents which have thus been rescued from forgetfulness, and the latest and most authoritative renderings of the texts.

The latest discovery of interest to the student of the Old Testament has been announced from Berlin. Among the tablets from Tel el-Amarna which have been acquired for the Museum at Berlin, five are found to have been despatches sent from the king or governor of Jerusalem to the kings of Egypt. I had already recognised the name of Uru'salim or "Jerusalem" in a tablet now in Cairo (*Academy*, 19th April 1890, p. 273); the tablets at Berlin give us further and unexpected information in regard to the later capital of the Judæan kingdom. In the fifteenth century before our era Jerusalem was governed by a certain Abdi-dhaba, or Ebed-tob as his name would have been written in Hebrew; and it is his letters which have just been deciphered by the German Assyriologists. He claims to have occupied a more independent position than the governors of the other cities of Palestine at the time. They were merely Egyptian officials, whereas he, though owning allegiance to the Egyptian monarch, claims to have been appointed to his office by "the oracle of the mighty king." This "mighty king" is shown by one of the despatches to have been the deity who was worshipped at Jerusalem. Abdi-dhaba, accordingly, must have been a priest-king like Melchizedek, "the priest of the most high God." A broken tablet which I copied in M. Bouriant's collection tells us what was the local name of the deity in question. Here we read: *al sad Uru'salim-*KI *al bit* AN NIN-IP: *sumu Mar-ruv al sarri padarat asar nisi al Kilti-*KI, "the city of the Mountain of Jerusalem, the city of the temple of the god Uras, (whose) name (there is) Marru, the city of the king, *defending*(?) the locality of the men of the city of Keilah." Consequently "the most high God," of whom Abram was blessed, was locally known under the name of *Marru*, which seems to be connected with the Aramaic *marê*, "lord," and was identified with the Babylonian Uras, the Eastern Sun. It is possible that the name of the god may throw light on that of Moriah, "the mountain" on which his sanctuary was erected.

Abdi-dhaba describes himself as having had dealings with the Kassi or Babylonians, and in one of his letters he says: "so long as a ship crosses the sea—this is the oracle of the mighty king—so long shall there be a continuance of the conquests of Nahrima and the Babylonians." Nahrima represents the Aram Naharaim of Scripture, and it is interesting to find that the conquests of a king of that country were known and feared in southern Palestine a hundred years before Israel was oppressed by Chushan-rish-athaim, the king of Aram Naharaim (Judg. iii. 8-10). The mention of the Babylonians is also interesting since Manetho avers that when the Hyksos were expelled from Egypt they built Jerusalem as a defence against the "Assyrians." In the age of Manetho "Assyrians" and "Babylonians" were synonymous terms.

While we are thus learning the inner history of Palestine in the century before the Israelitish invasion, the history of the fall of the Assyrian empire, late as it comparatively is in time, is still shrouded in obscurity. Two new facts only have been acquired of recent years in regard to it. One is that the Assyrian king whose name was doubtfully restored as [Bel-sum-]iskun was really called Sin-sar-iskun; the other is that Assur-etil-ilâni-yukinni, the son and successor of Assur-bani-pal, was acknowledged in northern Babylonia as late as the 4th year of his reign, tablets of that date having been found at Niffer by the American expedition. Since Sinsar-iskun seems evidently to be the Sarakos of Abydênos and Alexander Polyhistor, we must regard him as the last king of Assyria, of whom it was said that he had burnt himself to death in his palace. But between Assur-etil-ilâni-yukinni and Sin-sar-iskun it would appear that there was at least one king, possibly two. A tablet (K 195) was discovered by Mr. George Smith from which he translates the following passage: "Sin-inadina-pal son of Assur-akh-iddin (Esar-haddon), king of Assyria, whose name on this tablet is inscribed, to the government in the earth, in the presence of thy great divinity Shamas great lord, he is proclaimed and established."[1] The name of Sin-inadina-pal, or rather Sin-iddina-pal, reminds us of the classical Sardanapallos, and the tablet on which his name occurs belongs to a peculiar group, distinguished from all others in the Kouyunyik collection by their style of writing and expression. They begin with the words: "O Sun-god, great lord, I beseech thee; remove (our) sin."

Two tablets of this group (K 4668 and S 2005) were published by myself for the first time in 1877, in the Appendix to my *Babylonian Literature* (pp. 78-82).[2] I there pointed out that they belong to the closing days of the Assyrian Empire, and that

[1] *History of Assurbanipal*, p. 324.
[2] See *Records of the Past*, xi. first series, pp. 79-84. Other tablets belonging to the same group are K 1370, S 284, and S 2002.

the Esar-haddon mentioned in them must be a later king than the Esar-haddon otherwise known to history. I have since seen no reason to change my opinion. Before examining their contents, however, it is as well to translate such portions of them as give a continuous sense.

K 4668.

1. "O SUN-GOD, great lord, I beseech thee; O god of fixed destiny, remove [our] sin!
2. From this day, [from] the 3rd day of this month, even the month Iyyar, to the 15th day of Ab of this year,
3. for these 100 days (and) 100 nights religious ordinances (and) holy days the prophets have proclaimed in *writing* (?).
4. Whether Kastariti with his soldiers, or the soldiers of the GIMIRRÂ (Kimmerians),
5. or the soldiers of the MADÂ (Medes), or the soldiers of the MANNÂ (Minni), or (some other) enemy are capturing,
6. overflow, (and) plot, as to whether on the seventh day or . . .
7. or on a holy day with the weapons of war and combat, or with fire or engines that discharge bolts and missiles,
8. or with a *battering-ram* (?) or *siege* (?), or with famine,
9. or by oaths in the names of god and [king], or by . . . .
10. or by a covenant in writing they shall occupy the . . of the city.
11. The city of KISA'S'SU they have taken; a [trophy? in] the midst of the cities of KHARTAM (and) KISA'S'SU they erect:
12. the cities of KHARTAM (and) KISA'S'SU their hands capture.
13. Into their hands is delivered thy great divinity. The . . .

14. . . . of the cities of KHARTAM (and) KISA'S'SU the enemy sieze with the hands.
15. From this day to the day of the lesser feast, in the land, in the presence of thy great divinity
16. during the day within their . . . .
17. . . . . they plot, they return and . . . .

   .   .   .   .   .

26. Since that this day, even the 3rd day of this month Iyyar, until the 11th day of the month Ab of this year,
27. Kastariti with [his] soldiers, the soldiers of the GIMIRRÂ, the soldiers of the MANNÂ,
28. the soldiers of the MADÂ and [the enemy] are capturing,
29. the cities of KHARTAM (and) KISA'S'SU [they have taken], the cities of KHARTAM (and) KISA'S'SU they have entered,
30. the cities of KHARTAM (and) KISA'S'SU [their hands] capture; to their hands they are delivered."

S 2005.

1. "[O SUN-GOD], great [lord], I beseech thee, O god of fixed destiny remove [our sin]!
2. [Kas]tariti the lord of the city of KAR-KASSÎ, who to Mamiti-arsu
3. [the lord of the city] of the MADÂ sent, saying: We are confederate with one another, from the country [of ASSYRIA let us revolt.]
4. [Mami]ti-arsu listens; he is obedient; he sets his face
5. [to revolt] this year from Esar-haddon king [of ASSYRIA.]"

The rest of the tablet is too broken for translation, but mention is again made in it of "Mamitiarsu" or "Vavit-arsu," "the lord of the city of the Medes," and we are told that the city of Zaz was captured. Reference is also made in the tablets to the city of 'Sandu-litir and the 'Sapardâ or Sepharad of Obadiah (20), as well as to the fact that the enemy had "entered the city of Kilman."

The language of the tablets is not that of a powerful conqueror like Esar-haddon the son of Sennacherib. Moreover, the historical situation presupposed by them does not suit the history of his reign. He defeated the Gimirrâ on the northern frontier of his kingdom and drove them to the west. Their leader was Teuspa, not Kastarit, and he is called a Manda or "nomad." The Gimirrâ, furthermore, who were led by Teuspa, were not in alliance with the Medes or with any other of the populations of the north. The war of Esar-haddon with the Medes did not take place until long after the defeat of the Kimmerians, and so far were the Medes from being the aggressors that it was Esar-haddon who invaded their territory in the distant east. The Medes, in fact, were not yet in contact with the frontiers of Assyria. Finally, their leader was not Mamiti-arsu. The "city-lords" who were attacked and subjected by Esar-haddon bore the names of Sidirparna, Eparna, Uppiz, Zana'sana, and Ramateya. There is a plentiful choice of names here, but that of Mamiti-arsu does not appear among them.

On the other hand, the confederacy of which Kastarit was the head strikingly resembles that which is called upon in the prophecies of Jeremiah (li. 27, 28) to destroy the empire of Babylon. The prophet summons the "kingdoms of Ararat, Minni, and Ashkenaz," and "the kings of the Medes" to march upon Babylonia. Ararat or Van and Ashkenaz, the Assyrian Asguza, take the place of Kastarit and the Gimirrâ, but otherwise the situation is the same as that which is represented in the tablets. It is clear from Jer. l. 17, li. 34, that the prophecy was written while Nebuchadrezzar was still upon the throne of Babylon, and it would follow that the tablets which depict a similar political situation cannot belong to a much earlier date.

The Esar-haddon of the tablets, therefore, must be a later prince than Esar-haddon the father of Assur-bani-pal. The conclusion is confirmed by a tablet, published in *W. A. I.*, iii. 16, No. 2, which has been the subject of a special study by M. Amiaud.[1] It reads as follows: "Order of the daughter of the king to the lady Assur-sarrat. Now do not inscribe thy tablet, do not utter thy word, lest perhaps they say: 'This (is) the mistress of Serua-edherat, the eldest daughter of the harem of Assur-etil-ilâni-yukinni, the great king, the powerful king, the king of legions, the king of Assyria.' Yet thou (art) a mighty princess, the lady of the house of Assur-bani-pal, the eldest royal son of the harem of Esar-haddon king of Assyria." It would appear from these words that the wife of Assur-bani-pal, the eldest son of Esar-haddon, "king of Assyria," had attempted to assume authority over the dowager queen of Assur-etil-ilâni-yukinni. As the latter king

[1] "Esarhaddon II" in *The Babylonian and Oriental Record*, ii. 9.

was the successor of Assur-bani-pal, it is obvious that the Esar-haddon referred to in the tablet could not have been the father of Assur-bani-pal, and that the Assur-bani-pal whose wife was Assur-sarrat must have been a different prince from the famous Assyrian monarch. We must see in him a brother of Sin-iddina-pal, and it is possible that the Greek Sardanapallos has originated out of a fusion of the names of the two brothers Assur-(bani-pal) and (Sin)-iddina-pal.

However this may be, we must regard the existence of Esar-haddon II as an ascertained fact of history. Whether he was succeeded by one of his two sons Sin-iddina-pal and Assur-bani-pal II we do not know. All that seems clear is that between Assur-etil-ilâni-yukinni, the immediate successor of Assur-bani-pal, and Sin-sar-iskun the last Assyrian king there intervened the reign of Esar-haddon II, and that under him the foes of the empire first began to gather against it from the north-east. The king turned for help to the gods and the prophets; and the armies that had once made the name of Assyria terrible throughout the eastern world could no longer defend the cities they had garrisoned.

A. H. SAYCE.

QUEEN'S COLLEGE, OXFORD,
October 1890.

TABLE OF CONTENTS

		PAGE
I.	THE OFFICIAL LIFE OF AN EGYPTIAN OFFICER, PROM THE TOMB OF AMEN-EM-HEB AT THEBES. By PHILIPPE VIREY	
II.	HYMN TO OSIRIS ON THE STELE OF AMON-EM-HA. By D. MALLET	14
III.	THE SYNCHRONOUS HISTORY OF ASSYRIA AND BABYLONIA. By the EDITOR	24
IV.	INSCRIPTIONS OF SHALMANESER II (ON THE BLACK OBELISK, THE KURKH MONOLITH, AND THE GATES OF BALAWÂT). By the Rev. Dr. SCHEIL	36
V.	A VOTIVE INSCRIPTION OF ASSUR-NATSIR-PAL. By S. ARTHUR STRONG	80
VI.	INSCRIPTION OF RIMMON-NIRARI III. By S. ARTHUR STRONG	86
VII.	VOTIVE INSCRIPTIONS. By S. ARTHUR STRONG	90

		PAGE
VIII.	BABYLONIAN CONTRACT-TABLETS WITH HISTORICAL REFERENCES. By THEO. G. PINCHES	96
IX.	THE DEDICATION OF THREE BABYLONIANS TO THE SERVICE OF THE SUN-GOD AT SIPPARA. By the EDITOR	109
X.	THE GREAT INSCRIPTION OF ARGISTIS ON THE ROCK OF VAN. By the EDITOR	114
XI.	MONOLITH INSCRIPTION OF ARGISTIS KING OF VAN. By the EDITOR	134

EQUIVALENTS OF THE HEBREW LETTERS IN THE TRANS-
LITERATION OF ASSYRIAN NAMES MENTIONED IN
THESE VOLUMES.

א	a,	ל	l
ב	b	מ	m
ג	g	נ	n
ד	d	ס	's s
ה	h	ע	e
ו	u, v	פ	p
ז	z	צ	ts
ח	kh	ק	q
ט	dh	ר	r
י	i, y	ש	s, sh
כ	k	ת	t

N.B.—Those Assyriologists who transcribe ש by *sh* use *s* for ס. The Assyrian *e* represents a diphthong as well as ע.

In the Introductions and Notes W. A. I. denotes *The Cuneiform Inscriptions of Western Asia*, in five volumes, published by the Trustees of the British Museum. Doubtful words and expressions are followed by a note of interrogation, the preceding words being put into italics where necessary. *Lacunæ* are denoted by asterisks or by the insertion of supplied words between square brackets. Words needed to complete the sense in English, but not expressed in the original, are placed between round brackets. The names of individuals are distinguished from those of deities or localities by being printed in Roman type, the names of deities and localities being in capitals.

THE OFFICIAL LIFE OF AN EGYPTIAN OFFICER, FROM THE TOMB OF AMEN-EM-HEB AT THEBES

Translated by Philippe Virey

It is to Prof. Ebers that the honour belongs of having discovered and published this celebrated inscription, although Champollion before him had penetrated into the tomb of Amen-em-heb, of which he gives a short description in his *Notices*,[1] under No. 12. But the description is so summary that no inscription is noticed as existing in the tomb; nothing but the indication of the names of the defunct and his wife, and the mention of the cartouches of Thothmes III and Amenophis II allows us to affirm that it is really the tomb of Amen-em-heb. The monument, moreover, was buried in the sand, and had been completely forgotten when Prof. Ebers, during his stay at Thebes in 1872-73, had the good fortune to rediscover it. The great historical inscription contained in it attracted his attention, and he made a copy of the text, which he published in

[1] Page 505.

1873,[1] with a translation and interesting notes. My predecessors have already acknowledged the merits of this translation,[2] which can be appreciated by every Egyptologist. In my turn, I shall insist on the excellence of the copy, and I believe that I possess special qualifications for delivering such a judgment. Having myself had to transcribe all the texts in the tomb of Amen-em-heb,[3] I know well what difficulties Prof. Ebers has victoriously surmounted, and can recognise with what patience and sagacity he has made out the most obscure passages in a way that admits of no doubt, saving me from painful efforts and perhaps from unsuccessful conjectures.

If I now attempt to publish a new rendering of an inscription already translated by the masters of Egyptological science, it is that I wish to add a little sheaf of my own to the abundant harvest of facts collected at once by Prof. Ebers, and to put forward some new ideas derived from the study of other parts of the tomb of Amen-em-heb as well as of a neighbouring tomb belonging to an official of the same rank [4] as himself, entitled *tennu n suten tennu n menfiu* ("vicar of the king in the army," or substantially a minister of war). The great inscrip-

---

[1] *Zeit und Thaten Tothmes III*, in the *Zeitschrift für ægyptischer Sprache* (1873).

[2] Chabas, *Mélanges égyptologiques, 3me série*.

[3] They will appear in the *Mémoires publiés par les membres de la Mission archéologique française au Caire*.

[4] The tomb of Pehsukher. The contents of the tomb will be published along with those of the tomb of Amen-em-heb.

tion tells us in the first place what were the glorious services by which Amen-em-heb rose to so high a dignity.

What was the exact signification of his title? The word *tennu*, which Dr. Brugsch has carefully examined in the *Revue égyptologique*,[1] does not always signify a minister in the sense in which we ordinarily understand the word; but I hope to show that it certainly has this meaning in our inscription. It properly signifies, as ·Dr. Brugsch has pointed out, "a deputy," "a delegate," "a vicar." Prof. Maspero, in his *Manuel de Hiérarchie égyptienne*,[2] explains that the military chief of a nome had at his side a *tennu* of the troops, a lieutenant of the forces, who could act in his place, more particularly, as his title indicates, at the head of the troops who were in service, but probably also in the offices of the administration. The *tennu* or vicar of a military officer will therefore be his lieutenant; the *tennu* or vicar of the governor of a city will be an assistant governor; the *tennu* or vicar of the Chancellor[3] will perhaps be an under-secretary of state; but the vicar of the king will be a minister. I have elsewhere[4] come to the conclusion that the *tennu* of the troops, who in the provinces was only a sort of administrative officer or military intendant, was at Thebes, under the title of *tennu n*

---
[1] I. pp. 22 *sq.*   [2] Page 37.
[3] Examples are cited by Dr. Brugsch.
[4] In my work on the tomb of Rekhmara, Governor of Thebes under the eighteenth dynasty, p. 8, in the *Mémoires publiés par les membres de la Mission archéologique française au Caire*, v. (1889).

suten,[1] the deputy of the king, an actual minister of war. We see from the paintings which represent the conscription that he received recruits from all countries; in the tomb of Pehsukher many of them are Nubians and negroes. It was then the royal army which was administered by this functionary, but the royal army with the auxiliaries as distinct from the provincial contingents. In the different inscriptions of the tomb Amen-em-heb is further distinguished by a series of titles, all of which are thoroughly applicable to a minister of the king. But the most conclusive example is found in line 46 of our inscription, where the king says to Amen-em-heb: "Advance in dignity; be *tennu* of the army; and from the moment that this is said, watch over the royal forces." These words can have been addressed only to a minister; the meaning of "military intendant" is impossible here, for Amen-em-heb was already in command of the royal guard[2] when the king appointed him *tennu*, saying to him, "*Advance* in dignity." It would not have been an advancement for the commander of the guard to be appointed military intendant. I should add that Dr. Brugsch sees in the *tennu* or *aten* "of the world" and "of the two worlds" a sort of viceroy of Egypt or prime minister of the Pharaoh, and that Chabas remarks that there were *atennu* of foreign countries, of the treasury, and of the private house of the

---

[1] The example is taken from the tomb of Pehsukher.
[2] End of line 33 of the great inscription.

Pharaoh: "We recognise among them ministers of protected states, of finance, etc." The *tennu Mahu*, who was charged with the installation of Amen-em-heb,[1] was perhaps one of these ministers, but the text does not state what was the department which he administered. Sometimes, moreover, we find the terms *tennu n suten*, *tennu n hon-f* ("minister of the king," "minister of his majesty,"), without any further explanation.

In his new office Amen-em-heb superintended the recruiting of the army as well as its discipline and instruction. Several of the scenes depicted on the walls of his tomb represent him in the exercise of these functions. We notice among them a document which gives us a high idea of the organisation of the Egyptian troops, and enables us to understand their superiority to the hordes of Asia. "Behold the arm of Egypt,"[2] says Amen-em-heb to the king, pointing out to him at the same time the officers who defiled before him: "behold the numerous force which is under thy hand. We form a complete whole, having but one mouth, one arm, one hand, all of us, the soldiers [keeping their ranks (?)],[3] and none quitting them."

The maintenance of the troops, accordingly, depended on the superior direction of the *tennu*. We see him presenting the officers of the commissariat to the king. "He causes the officers of the adminis-

---

[1] Line 46. [2] Literally "the smiter of the double earth."
[3] Illegible

tration of the army, the officers of the commissariat, to march past before the Pharaoh, in order that the sacks may be filled with provisions, bread, beef, wine, biscuits, all sorts of vegetables, and all good things."

The tomb of Pehsukher shows us even the operations of harvest, in districts doubtless appropriated to the maintenance of the army, and sets before us a scene representing the inspection of the magazines of food. A clerk sums up the amount, and certain officers taste the quality of the provisions. The *tennu* thus has at his disposal a numerous administrative staff, and is at the same time at the head of the army. The officers who presented themselves before him were first of all received by the "scribe of the writings or the secretary of the *tennu*." And in a transport of pride the latter exclaimed: "There is none greater than myself! There is none greater than myself!"[1] thus asserting that he held the first rank among men, and next to the monarch who represented the divinity, and whose minister he consequently was.

[1] Stêlê of Pehsukher, line 23.

men as prisoners, alive. When his majesty reached NAHARAIN[1]

5. I brought thither the three men as booty, whom I placed before thy[2] majesty, as living prisoners.
6. Another time[3] I captured (it was in the expedition[4] to the country of mount UAN, to the west of ALEPPO[5]), and I brought back
7. (certain) captured Asiatics, as living prisoners 13 men, 70 asses alive,[6] 13 basons of iron, . . . basons of worked gold. . . .
8. . . . Another time I captured (it was in an expedition to the country of CARCHEMISH[7]) and brought away . . .
9. . . . . . . as living prisoners. I traversed the water of NAHARAIN[8] without letting them escape,[9]
10. [and] I [set] them before my master. Behold, there-

have interfered with his operations to look to their own defence, and prevented others from joining in the revolt. Amen-em-heb was in one of these columns, and consequently his first exploits in the countries of Nekeb, Uan, and Carchemish took place at a distance from the king.

[1] The Aram-Naharaim, or Aram of the two rivers, of the Old Testament (Judges iii. 8), placed by Prof. Maspero between the Euphrates and the Orontes. [The tablets of Tel el-Amarna, however, show that the chief seat of the king of Naharain was on the eastern bank of the Euphrates, opposite Carchemish, as they identify the Naharain of the Egyptian monuments with the country of Mitanni, whose position is known from the Assyrian inscriptions.—ED.]
[2] Amen-em-heb addresses his inscription to the deified Thothmes III.
[3] Literally "anew."
[4] Literally "this expedition to the land of Mount Uan."
[5] Kharbu or Khalep. The expedition probably took place while Thothmes was besieging Aleppo. Help might have been sent to Aleppo from the land of the Hittites on the north-west, which would explain the despatch of an Egyptian force in this direction.
[6] Or perhaps "heads" or "beings," equivalent to *sa* ("human being").
[7] Doubtless during the siege of Aleppo, to which Carchemish was near. [Carchemish, the Hittite capital, was situated on the western bank of the Euphrates, a little to the north of its junction with the Sajur, and is now represented by the mounds of Jerablûs, from which Hittite sculptures and inscriptions have been brought to the British Museum. Its fortifications on the river-side are depicted on the bronze gates of Balawât. It commanded the great ford over the Euphrates, and the defeat of the Egyptian Pharaoh under its walls established the empire of Nebuchadnezzar in Western Asia (Jer. xlvi. 2).—ED.] [8] Probably the Euphrates.
[9] Literally "they being in my hand."

fore, he rewarded me with a great reward, namely
. . . .

11. . . . . I saw the victory of the king, the king of the south and of the north, even Ra-men-kheper,[1] the life-giver, in the country of SENZAR.[2] He made . . .

12. . . . . them. There I captured before the king and I brought back a hand.[3] He gave me the gold of guerdon, namely

13. 2 rings [of gold] and silver. When I began again to behold his valour, I was among his bodyguard,[4] at the capture of

14. KADESH,[5] without quitting the place which was under him. I brought back of the Marinas[6] 2 personages as [living prisoners].

15. before the king, the lord of the two worlds,[7] Thothmes . . . who gives life eternally. He gave me gold for my valour in the presence of the master,

16. namely the collar of the lion of gold, 2 *shebi* collars, 2 helmets and 4 bracelets. And I saw my master . .

17. . . . . . .

18. . . . . . . HA;[8] then afresh [it was] overthrown.[9] As for me, I ascended towards . . . . . .

19. I began again to see his valour in the country of TAKHIS;[10] . . . . . -

---

[1] That is to say, Thothmes III.

[2] According to Chabas the district on the left bank of the Euphrates, adjoining that of Aleppo and Carchemish. Henceforth Amen-em-heb remained in the corps commanded by the king; after the first siege of Kadesh he was among the body-guard. His admission into them was the reward of his first exploits.

[3] Perhaps the hand of an enemy slain in single combat.

[4] Literally "his followers."

[5] [Subsequently the southern capital of the Hittites, on the Orontes close to the modern Bahr el-Qadis, or Lake of Qadis, westward of Homs.—ED.]   [6] Or "chiefs."

[7] Or "the double earth," that is Egypt.

[8] Some country is doubtless referred to which was protected by its distance from Egypt, and after the withdrawal of the Egyptian forces was therefore able to recover its independence. Thothmes spread terror by the suddenness of his appearance in the most distant quarters.

[9] I imagine that the country whose name is lost is here meant.

[10] Amenophis II subsequently punished a revolt of this country [which lay near the Orontes].

20. I captured there before the king and brought away (certain) Asiatics 3 men [1] alive as prisoners. Then
21. my lord gave me the gold of guerdon, namely, 2 collars, 4 bracelets [with] 2 helmets [and] a tame [2] lion.
22. I began again to see another perfect action performed by the master of the two worlds in the country of Nii.[3] He took in hunting 120 elephants for their tusks. . . .
23. The largest among them attempted to fight face to face [4] with his majesty. As for me, I cut off his foot,[5] although he was alive . . . .
24. . . . . . . I entered for thee [6] into the water which is between the two stones [7]; then my master rewarded me with gold.
25. . . . . . . Behold, the prince of KADESH drove [8] a mare
26. straight against . . . . as it charged among the soldiers I hurried to meet it [9]
27. on foot, with my dagger, [and] I opened its stomach. I cut off its tail [and] made of it a trophy [10]
28. in the royal work of giving thanks to God because thereof.[11] That caused joy to take possession of my heart [and] cheerfulness to alight upon my limbs.[12]

---

[1] Prof. Ebers's copy has "women."   [2] Literally "slave."
[3] Not Nineveh, but, as Prof. Maspero has pointed out, a locality in northern Syria.
[4] Literally "facing." The elephant turned against the king and charged upon him.
[5] Literally "hand"; either the front foot or the trunk.
[6] That is, the king.
[7] Perhaps a dangerous passage where Amen-em-heb showed his courage, or, as Chabas suggested, the two stelæ erected by Thothmes III on the two sides of the Euphrates to mark the western limit of his empire.
[8] Literally "caused a mare to go out against."
[9] Literally "I was hurrying myself against it."
[10] Literally "I arranged it."
[11] Probably the mare had caused confusion in the Egyptian ranks, so that the king gave thanks to God for deliverance from peril.
[12] These events occurred in the forty-second year of the reign of Thothmes III. The prince of Kadesh, whose capital had already been captured (lines 13-14) in the thirtieth year of his reign, and its walls razed, had revolted after having rebuilt his fortifications. Hence Amen-em-heb

29. His majesty despatched the most valiant of his soldiers to force the newly-constructed rampart of KADESH. It was I who
30. forced it, for I was in advance of the most valiant; no other [was] before me. When I left (it) I brought back (with me) of the Marinas[1]
31. 2 personages as living prisoners. My master began again to reward me because of this with every sort
32. of good thing,[2] for it was pleasing to the king that I had made this capture.[3] Being an officer . . . . .
33. it was I who directed the manœuvre in . . . . as captain of his body-guard.
34. . . . . . . in his fair festival of Apet, when men [were] full of joy . . . . . .
35. Behold for the king, the age he passed[4] of years abundant and happy, as a strong man, as a . . . .
36. as a truth-speaker,[5] from his happy first year until his 54th year, the last day of the month Phamenoth.[6] Then the king of the south and of the north,
37. Ra-men-kheper, the truth-speaker, ascended to heaven, to unite himself with the solar disk, and to follow God, who penetrates when he makes himself luminous
38. under the form of the solar disk which illuminates the sky at the same time that it shines. The king of

speaks of "the newly-constructed rampart of Kadesh." But before shutting himself up in the city the prince offered battle, and employed the stratagem which was baffled by Amen-em-heb.

[1] Or "chiefs."
[2] No doubt there were no more decorations for Amen-em-heb to desire.
[3] After the second capture of Kadesh Syria submitted, and the campaigns of Amen-em-heb under Thothmes came to an end. Henceforth he commanded the royal bodyguard in Egypt, where the king resided after the conclusion of his wars.
[4] Literally "behold the king as to the duration of his time in years." The campaigns of Thothmes ended, Amen-em-heb has nothing more to record.
[5] *Mâ-kheru* ("whose voice makes true," or "realises," the privilege, in the first place, of the deity and then of the deified dead). The king is also *mâ-kheru*, because he realises the designs of the deity whose incarnation he is upon the earth.
[6] The third month of winter.

the south and of the north, Ra-ââ-khepru, the son of the Sun, Amen-hotep,[1] the giver of life,

39. establishing himself on the throne of his father, reduced under the royal banner all that made opposition to him. He pierced the wretches[2] . . . . . .

40. and of the desert; he immolated their chiefs, rising like HORUS[3] the son of ISIS, taking possession of . . . . . .

41. . . . . . . *the extremity* (?) of all those who exist and breathe, all the mountain and plain, bowed as it were before his wishes, their tributes on their backs.[4]

42. [He] granted unto them the breath of life. Behold his majesty saw me sailing with him in his bark

43. named Khâ-m-suten-uaa, while I was at . . . . of the fair festival of Apet-rest, conformably to custom.[5]

44. . . . . . . when I re-ascended, even I, into the interior of the palace, an order [was given] to stand in the presence [of the king] . . . . Ra-ââ-khepru; it was

45. a great honour. I flew, even I, on the spot, into the presence of his majesty. He said to me : " I know thy conduct . . . . . .

---

[1] Amenophis II.
[2] The new king is compared with the rising sun, which pierced with its rays the shadows where the evil principles hide themselves. A revolt seems to have broken out at the time among the desert tribes, who are likened to the race of Set or Typhon, the god of aridity.
[3] The result of the comparison between the new king and the rising sun.
[4] This is represented in three pictures below the inscription. The upper picture shows us, according to the epigraph, "all the princes of Upper RUTENNU, who proclaim : Great are thy desires ; thou puttest fear in all the double land (of EGYPT), and all [foreign lands are] under thy sandals." One prince is prostrate ; two others, on their knees, extend their arms in supplication ; a fourth, standing, presents a vase ; a fifth, also standing, offers suppliantly a small child whom he holds in his arms ; another child is in front of him. A sixth chief also brings a child. Other persons follow of different physiognomies and head-dresses ; but owing to the mutilation of the wall the end of the scene is indistinct. In the second picture are "all the chiefs of Lower RUTENNU ;" but the scene represented in it does not differ from that of the first picture. The legend attached to the third picture is almost entirely effaced. A person is represented in it prostrate and accompanied by three others who are kneeling, and two more who carry vases of various forms. Beyond this the wall is mutilated.
[5] As had been the case under Thothmes. Amen-em-heb means that he preserved his old functions.

46. serving my father. Advance in dignity; be *tennu* of the army; and from the moment that this is said watch over the royal forces." The *tennu* Mahu[1] executed all his words.[2]

[1] For the meaning of this title see the Introduction.
[2] *Zettu nebu-f.* I think the form *zettu-f nebu* or *nebt* would be more regular. Perhaps we should read *zettu neb-f* ("the words of his master"), and suppose that the Egyptian artist has committed an error in copying the inscription from a hieratic original, by confusing the determinative of *neb* ("master") with the sign of the plural.

HYMN TO OSIRIS ON THE STELE OF AMON-EM-HA

TRANSLATED BY D. MALLET

THIS hymn to Osiris is engraved on a semi-circular stele of limestone which forms part of the collection of the Bibliothèque Nationale at Paris. It comprises 28 lines of hieroglyphics, in a very good state of preservation, excepting only that the name of the god Amon, which once figured in several proper names, has been carefully chiselled out, in the age of the so-called heretic kings Khu-n-Aten (Amenophis IV) and his successors.

The text may have been sculptured on the stele in the time of the eighteenth dynasty—Chabas has remarked that the wife of Amon-mes, the father of Amon-em-ha, bore the same name as the favourite wife of Amenophis I—but it reproduces a religious work of more ancient date, which goes back at least to the epoch of the twelfth dynasty, as is shown on the one hand by the small number of determinatives and on the other by the use of certain formulæ, *e.g.* the position of the father's name before that of the son : " Osiris son Horus" in the sense of "Horus son of Osiris." The references of the monument to the cult of Osiris are consequently very ancient, and they thus possess all the greater importance for the history of the Egyptian religion.

The text has been reproduced for the first time and translated by Chabas in the *Revue archéologique* (May-June 1857), from a squeeze furnished him by Devéria. Chabas published a new translation, which differed considerably from the first, in the first series of *Records of the Past*, vol. vi. pp. 99 *sqq*.

The semicircular part of the stele is divided into two compartments. At the top is the ring in the form of a seal, accompanied by the two sacred eyes. The first compartment includes two scenes of unequal importance. On the left, Amon-em-ha presents the table of offerings, filled with provisions of all sorts, to his father and mother, seated side by side in a large armchair, the wife resting the left hand, as usual, on the shoulder of her husband. Behind the chair is a child, with a long lock of hair, who puts his left hand to his mouth and holds a flower in the right. Behind him runs a vertical inscription : " His son Amon-em-ua." Above the two seated personages we read : " The superintendent of the oxen Amon-mes ; his wife, the mistress of the house, Nofri-t-ari." Above the table of offerings is : " His son Amon-em-ha." On the right, a person clothed in a panther's skin, the characteristic garb of the priests, presents a seated lady, "the mistress Baki-t, deceased "—doubtless another wife of Amon-mes—

with an incense-burner which has a long handle like an arm, while with the other hand he pours out a libation of water over a double altar, and the legend engraved before him runs : " The Khri-heb of Osiris, the son, comes."

The second compartment is occupied by a series of six kneeling persons, whose faces are turned to the right ; their names are engraved in a vertical direction in front of each of them :—" His son Si-t-Maut ; his son Amon-ken ; his daughter Meri-t; his daughter Amon-bai-t ; his daughter Suten-Maut; his daughter Hui-em-nuter."

Next comes the hymn itself, which occupies the rest of the stele.

HYMN TO OSIRIS

1. Adoration to OSIRIS by the superintendent of the oxen, Amon-em-ha son of the lady Nofri-t-ari. He says: Homage to thee, OSIRIS, lord of eternity, king of the gods with the thousand names,[1] with the sacred existences,[2] with the secret acts[3] in the temples; he is rich in *Ka*[4] in TATTU,[5] holding property[6]

2. in SOKHEM,[7] master of the sacred dances[8] in BUSIRIS, prince of abundance[9] in ON,[10] master of remembrance in MATI,[11] hidden soul, master of KERER,[12] venerated in the MEMPHITE nome;[13] the soul whose body itself is RA, who reposes in

---

[1] Compare the epithet "with a myriad of names" often applied to Isis by the Greeks (Plutarch: *de Isid. et Osirid.* 53). A Greek inscription in the Louvre (No. 1) calls her "many-named." The same expression is used of Amon.

[2] *Kheperu* is usually translated here "transformations." But Osiris is never transformed and *khoper* merely signifies "to be" or "become."

[3] *Ar-u* or *ir-u* has no determinative; it appears to refer to the ceremonies performed in the temples rather than to the forms of the god.

[4] The *Ka* is the double of the individual; the gods and sometimes men themselves have several; at Mendes Osiris doubtless had quite a series of them inherent in his sacred statues.

[5] Mendes.   [6] Or perhaps, "great nourisher."

[7] Letopolis.

[8] The word is several times determined in this stele by the figure of a dancing man, so that it must refer to dances in the temple performed in honour of the god.

[9] Literally "provisions of victualling."

[10] Heliopolis, the On of the Old Testament, the daughter of whose priest was married by Joseph.

[11] Unidentified locality. It is the name of the Hall of Truth where Osiris and his assessors judge the souls of the dead.

[12] Perhaps Paqrur, Phagroriopolis. In the tomb of Bok-en-ranf near Saqqarah, Osiris also is named "master of Kerer"; in the temple of Seti I. at Qurnah, Anubis has the same title.   [13] "The White Wall."

3. HNES;[1] dispensing benefits[2] in NART,[3] when his soul awakens, master of the great dwelling of SHMUN,[4] very valiant[5] in SHASHOTEP,[6] lord of eternity, the first in ABYDOS; distant is his domain in TO-SAR,[7] stable is

4. his name in the mouth of mankind; he who contains the double ennead of the double land; TUM who nourishes the doubles, first of the divine ennead, perfect ghost among the ghosts.[8] The NU[9] has procured for him his water,[10] the wind of the north has brought him food,[11] the air enters his nostrils, to refresh his heart,

5. to strengthen his heart.[12] The soil has produced for him provisions, the vault of heaven has brought[13] unto him its stars; the wide gates open for him, the master of acclamations in the southern sky, of adorations in the northern sky. The indestructible ones

6. are under the place of his face, the immortals are his abodes.[14] When he has gone forth in peace by the

---

[1] Herakleopolis, now the mounds of Ahnas el-Medineh, S.E. of the Fayoum. It is the Hanes of the Old Testament (Isai. xxx. 4).

[2] Literally "beneficent in useful things: *hannu* here has no determinative.

[3] A locality near Hanes and often identified with the latter.

[4] Hermopolis Magna. [5] Literally "great with the double solar force."

[6] Shotb, capital of the Hypselite nome, S. of Assiout.

[7] "The sacred land."

[8] *Khu*, "luminous," and hence "a magic power," often applied to the dead as having become luminous.

[9] The primordial water or abyss. Compare "the deep" of Gen. i. 2.

[10] *Khenp* is usually rendered "to extract." But the Nu is anterior to Osiris, and therefore gives instead of receiving his water. Moreover the construction seems to make this explanation necessary.

[11] *Meses*, "the night," more especially that which precedes the New Year, and hence the feast which took place then in honour of Osiris (Brugsch, *Dict.*, 700).

[12] Perhaps the word I have read *rut-u* should be decomposed into *rtu renpet-i-u*, "to give the productions of the year (to his heart)."

[13] Or "has submitted to him."

[14] The two compound words in parellelism here, *akhim-u sek-u, akhim-u urtt-u*, have been translated: "the fixed stars" and "the wandering stars" or planets, as well as "stars which always remain on the horizon," and "stars which are there only at certain hours." These distinctions are not proved; and it is best to adhere to the literal sense of the words.

order of SEB, the divine ennead adores him, the inhabitants of the *tuau*[1] prostrate themselves to the ground, the mighty[2] bow the head, the ancestors[3] are in prayer.

7. When they beheld him, the august dead[4] submit to him, the two lands together[5] unite to render glory to him, marching before his majesty. Glorious noble among the nobles[6] from whom proceeds [all] dignity, who establishes supreme authority,[7] excellent chief of the ennead of the gods, with charming aspect,

8. beloved of him who has contemplated him, extending his terror through all countries that they may proclaim his name before all others.[8] All make offerings unto him, even to him the master whose memory (is eternal) in heaven as on the earth. Manifold are the shouts during the festival of Uaga[9]; the two lands are united to celebrate the funeral dances.[10]

9. The great prince, eldest of his brothers, the chiefs[11] ot the divine enneads, who establishes the truth in the

---

[1] The other world, which in Egyptian belief was not *under* the earth but beyond its limits ; see Maspero, *Revue de l'Histoire des Religions*, 1887.

[2] The word read *t'at'a-u* by Chabas seems to be *tes-ti-u*, "those who are exalted," and forms a natural antithesis to *kes-u*, "bent."

[3] *T'er-ti-u* and not *t'era-u* ("all"), that is the common herd of the dead, the ancestors of men in general, in opposition to the *tes-ti-u* or "mighty."

[4] *Nti-u am*, "those who are below," a vague expression, euphemistic for "the dead." [5] Literally "in a single place."

[6] *Sahu* probably denotes the higher officials.

[7] *Hiq* is a feudal prince, and *hiq-t* the absolute authority he possessed in his domain, large or small, whether composed of several nomes or of less extent than a single nome. The title is often applied to the kings, though not as kings of all Egypt.

[8] Literally "in advance."

[9] One of the great festivals of Osiris when lamps were lit throughout Egypt (see Herodotos ii. 62).

[10] *Ahi* is, like *hannu*, determined by the figure of a dancing man. As the festival was in honour of the dead, the dances would have had a funereal character.

[11] *Ur-u* is in the plural, and consequently must be construed with the preceding word.

double land, who seats the son on the throne of his father, the favourite of his father SEB, the beloved of his mother NUT; very valiant, he overthrows the impious; strong of arm, he immolates

10. his adversary, breathing terror upon his enemies, conquering the distant frontiers of the wicked.[1] Firm of heart, his feet are vigilant. Flesh [2] of SEB, royalty [3] of the two lands, [SEB] contemplates his benefits, he has ordered him to govern

11. [all] countries to assure their prosperity.[4] He has fashioned this earth with his hand, [with] its waters, its atmosphere, its vegetation, all its large cattle, all its wild birds, all its domesticated birds,[5] its reptiles and its game.

12. The desert carries its tribute to the son of NUT, EGYPT is happy when it sees him appear on the throne of his father. Like RA he rises on the horizon, he creates light on the face of the darkness; he has illuminated SHU [6] by the help of his two feathers, he has inundated the earth like

13. the (solar) disk at dawn. His white crown pierces the vault of heaven fraternising with the stars, guides [7] of all the gods. Accomplished are the commands of his voice; [for he is the] favourite of the great ennead, the chosen of the small divine ennead. His sister has saved him, scattering the rebels,

14. repelling [8] evil, uttering the word with the incantations [9]

---

[1] Literally, "bringing on the frontiers," often applied to conquering kings.   [2] Or "heir."
[3] As in English, abstract terms are sometimes used of persons.
[4] Literally, "to conduct the countries to prosperity."
[5] *Pai* are the birds who fly freely through the air, *khenen* those who rest, probably therefore domestic fowls or perhaps water-fowl.
[6] Shu sometimes means "the shade," but here it seems to denote either the god Shu himself or the space which he occupies between the earth and the sky, uplifting, like Atlas, the celestial vault with his two arms.
[7] *Sem-u* also signifies "image," a sense which would suit here very well, the stars being images or manifestations of each god. The absence of a determinative makes a decision difficult.
[8] "Making turn," literally.
[9] *Khu*, the magic charms which enable the gods and more especially Isis to triumph.

of her mouth. Expert is her tongue, voice is not wanting to her, and her speech is effectual. [For she is] Isis the charmer, the avenger of her brother, who seeks him without failing,

15. who traverses this earth with lamentations, without resting [1] before she has found him, creating the light with her feathers, producing the wind with her wings, celebrating the sacred dances and depositing her brother in the tomb,

16. raising [2] the remains of the god with the immovable heart; [3] inhaling his seed, making flesh, [4] suckling the infant [5] in solitude without any knowing where he is. [6] She makes him grow, his arm becomes strong in the great dwelling

17. of SEB. The divine ennead rejoices, when the son of OSIRIS comes, even HORUS [7] with the firm heart, with the just voice, [8] the son of ISIS, the flesh of OSIRIS. He has assembled the chiefs of truth, [9] the divine ennead, [he] himself the universal master. [10] The lords of truth collected there

18. cast sin afar from them, [11] seated in the vast dwelling-place of SEB, to establish the dignity of him who is their master, the royalty of justice who resides there. HORUS has been found of just voice; to him has been given the office of his father. The diadem has come to him by the order of SEB;

---

[1] *Khen* used of birds who remain stationary. Elsewhere Isis is winged.
[2] Putting them one on the other so as to reconstitute the mutilated body of Osiris.   [3] That is Osiris.   [4] Or "an heir."
[5] Horus, born of Isis and the revivified Osiris.
[6] Isis hid herself in the marshes of the Delta with Horus in order to rear him in peace.
[7] In the text "Osiris son Horus." This way of expressing affiliation belongs to the age of the twelfth dynasty, *e.g.* in the tomb of Khnum-hotep at Beni-Hassan, where we have "Neheri son Khnum-hotep," *i.e.* Khnum-hotep son of Neheri (Cf. Lepsius, *Denkmäler*, iv. pl. 126 *sqq.*).
[8] M. Maspero explains this expression, which is used generally of the defunct, in a material sense, "he whose voice knows the correct intonation in reciting prayers and formulæ." M. Grébaut and most Egyptologists take it in a moral sense: "true of speech," "truth speaking."
[9] The acolytes who sit with Osiris in the Hall of Truth.
[10] Perhaps this merely signifies "the entire god" who now has all his limbs.   [11] Literally "put behind them."

19. he has assumed the dominion of the double land, the white crown being established on his head. He has valued¹ the earth with all it contains; heaven and earth are under the place of his face;² [SEB] has made him command mankind, the spirits,³ the race of the men of EGYPT, the HA-NEB-U.⁴ The circle

20. of the solar disk is under his orders, winds, river, inundation, fruit trees⁵ as well as all the annual plants.

As the god NEPRI⁶ he makes all his herbage, the wealth of the soil, to grow; he ascends and all are satiated; he spreads⁷ himself through all lands.

21. All that exists breathes; (all) hearts are happy, (all) breasts rejoice. Every being invokes him, every man adores his beauties. Delightful for us is his love; his grace environs the heart; great is his love in all the reins. One offers

22 unto the son of ISIS his enemy overthrown by his vigour. The author of evil pronounces magical words and displays his power in his turn;⁸ [but] the son of ISIS makes his way unto him, he avenges his father, sanctifying and honouring⁹ his name. Terror is calmed;

23. her domain is extended, is strengthened according to the laws which he¹⁰ dictates. The paths are cleared, the roads are opened, evil flies away; the earth,

---

¹ Properly, "count," "reckoning." The same metaphor occurs in the Bible.
² Compare the Biblical expression in Psalm lx. 13.
³ *Rekhi-u* "the intelligent," "those who know," frequently used of the dead.
⁴ "All those of the north,' *i.e.* 'all the inhabitants of the islands and coasts of the Mediterranean. In later times the term was specially used of the Greeks.
⁵ Or perhaps "trees which last," in opposition to plants which die and revive each year.
⁶ The grain-god who presided over cereals, vegetation, and the products of the earth. Amon-Ra is also called Nepri in the hymn contained in the Bulaq Museum (pl. viii. Grébaut, *Hymne à Amon-Ra*, p. 21).
⁷ Properly, "every face."   ⁸ Literally "his time."
⁹ Or "rendering beneficent."   ¹⁰ Horus or Osiris.

fertilised by its lord, teems[1] with produce. Established is the truth

24. for its master; sin is pursued; happy is thy heart, O UNNOFRÉ.[2] The son of ISIS has assumed the white crown, he has caused the authority of his father to be recognised in the great dwelling of SEB. RA is his word, THOTH are his writings.

25. The divine chiefs[3] are happy, [for] what thy father SEB has ordained for thee, that is executed when he has spoken.

Divine oblation to OSIRIS KHENT-AMENTI, lord of ABYDOS, so that he may give good funeral offerings of bread, liquids, oxen, geese, cloths, incense, perfumes

26. and all vegetable products; [so that he may grant] to grow,[4] to take possession of the NILE, to appear in the form of a living soul, to see the (solar) disk at dawn, to enter and depart by the *ro-sta-u*;[5] so that the soul may not be driven into the other world, but be received

27. among those who chant in the presence of UN-NOFRÉ and who share in the offerings laid upon the altar of the great god; so that it breathes the delicious breezes of the north and drinks of the current

28. of the river.

To the double of the superintendent of the oxen of AMON, Amon-mes, of the just voice, born of the lady Hont, of the just voice, his wife who loves him [Nofri-t-ari].

---

[1] The determinative of the legs seems to contradict this rendering, but I can find no other signification for the word *auru*, *wuru*, and we are compelled to admit a grammatical error. [2] "The good being," Osiris.
[3] Those who sit with Osiris in the Hall of Judgment.
[4] *Khopiru*, "the becomings."
[5] The corridors or defiles which led (like the defiles of the mountain-cliffs to the west of Abydos) from this world to the next.

THE SYNCHRONOUS HISTORY OF ASSYRIA AND BABYLONIA

TRANSLATED BY THE EDITOR

THE so-called Synchronous History of Assyria and Babylonia has been translated in part by myself in the former series of *Records of the Past*, iii. pp. 29-36. I see no reason for changing the translation given there; but as several new fragments of the history have been discovered since its publication, it is necessary that the document as we now have it should be placed before the reader. Its historical importance is considerable; not only are kings of Assyria and Babylonia mentioned in it with whose names we are otherwise unacquainted, but the order in which they occur, as well as their contemporaneity, is our only guide towards settling the chronology of the earlier period of Assyrian history.

A translation of the document has lately been published by Dr. Peiser and Dr. Winckler in the *Keilinschriftliche Bibliothek*, i. pp. 194-203. They are doubtless right in holding that it is not a history in the proper sense of the word, but a historical retrospect of the arrangements made by the Assyrian and Babylonian kings in regard to the disputed territory which lay between the two kingdoms. It formed part, in fact, of a legal statement of the case made on behalf of Assyria in the time of one of the immediate successors of Rimmon-nirari III. Hence the absence of dates which characterises it, as well as its reference only to those monarchs who in war or peace concerned themselves with the territory in question. The recently discovered tablets of Tel el-Amarna contain letters from Assur-yuballidh of Assyria and Burna-buryas of Babylonia to the Egyptian king, and they further show that the immediate predecessor of Burna-buryas was not Kara-indas but Ris-takullima-Sin. Since Shalmaneser I., whose date is fixed by an inscription of Sennacherib about 1300 B.C. (see *Records of the Past*, new series, vol. ii. p. 3, note 2), was the grandson of Pudil or Pediel, who was himself "the son of Bel-nirari the son of Assur-yuballidh," we may consider the last-named to have reigned about 1400 B.C.

The beginning of the document is lost, only the ends of the first eleven lines being preserved. These read as follows :

1. . . . . to (?) Assyria (*or* Assur)
2. . . . . his . . . .
3. . . . . . . before (?) him I speak
4. . . . .
5. . . . . . for future days
6. [I have indited] a memorial (tablet)
7. . . . . (of) the glory (and) power

8. [which the kings of Assyria have displayed] in that they overcame everything,
9. . . . (and of) the former campaigns
10. [in which foreign lands] were conquered
11. [and their spoil] brought back, and

. . . . . .

Another fragment of the text has also been found which Messrs. Peiser and Winckler believe should be inserted between col. iii. l. 36, and col. iv. l. 1. This reads :

1. . . . . . they fixed a common frontier
2. . . . . [Merodach-baladh-'su-iq]bi king of Kar-dunias
3. . . . . . . [Samas-]Rimmon king of Assyria
4. [defeated; Merodach-baladh-]'su-iqbi he destroyed [utterly],
5. [with the bodies of] his warriors he filled the field.

THE SYNCHRONOUS HISTORY OF ASSYRIA AND BABYLONIA

OBVERSE

COLUMN I.—THE COMMENCEMENT IS DESTROYED

1. Kara-indas king of KAR-DU[NIAS]
2. and Assur-bil-nisi-su king of ASSYRIA a covenant
3. between them with one another established;
4. and they gave an oath of their own accord[1] to one another in regard to the boundaries.

---

5. Buzur-Assur king of ASSYRIA and Burna-buryas
6. king of KAR-DUNIAS had a conference, and a definite
7. boundary they fixed of their own accord.

---

8. In the time of Assur-yuballidh king of ASSYRIA, Kara-Murudas
9. king of KAR-DUNIAS the son of Muballidhat-Serua
10. the daughter of Assur-yuballidh, soldiers of the KASSI[2]
11. revolted against and slew him. Nazi-bugas
12. [a man of] low parentage they raised to the kingdom to be over them.

---

13. [Bel-nirari to] exact vengeance

[1] The word has nothing to do with the pronoun *annu* as is supposed in Schrader's *Keilinschriftliche Bibliothek*.
[2] The Kassi or Kossæans were mountaineers who lived in Elam on the eastern side of Babylonia. They conquered Babylonia and there founded a dynasty to which Kara-Murudas belonged.

14. [for Kara-]Murudas¹ [his nephew] marched to KAR-DUNIYAS.
15. [Nazi-]bugas king of KAR-DU[NI]AS he slew;
16. [Kuri-]galzu the second, the son of Burna-buryas,
17. he appointed to the kingdom; on the throne of [his] father [he seated him].

---

18. In the time of Bel-nirari king of ASSYRIA Kuri-galzu the second² [king of KAR-DUNIAS]
19. with Bel-nirari king of ASSYRIA in the city of 'Sugagi which is upon the [TIGRIS]
20. fought. He utterly defeated him. His soldiers [he slew].
21. His camp he spoiled. From the *ascent* (?) to the land of SUBARI³
22. as far as the land of KAR-DUNIAS they neutralised⁴ the country and fixed (it);
23. a definite boundary they established.

---

24. Rimmon-nirari king of ASSYRIA⁵ (and) Nazi-Murudas king of KAR-DUNIAS
25. fought with one another in the city of KAR-ISTAR-AGAR'SALLU.⁶
26. Rimmon-nirari utterly overthrew Nazi-Murudas.
27. He shattered his forces;⁷ his camp (and) his tutelary gods⁸ he took from him.

---

¹ The text has *-indas*, but this is evidently an error of the scribe. Bel-nirari was the son of Assur-yuballidh and the great-grandfather of Shalmaneser I., who, we learn from an inscription of Sennacherib, was reigning about 1300 B.C.
² Or perhaps "the child." There seem to have been three kings of the name of Kuri-galzu.
³ This can hardly be the Subari or Subarti of the historical texts, which lay in the far north in the neighbourhood of Diarbekir. See vol. i. p. 99, note 1.   ⁴ Literally "caused to be alike" to both.
⁵ Rimmon-nirati I. was the grandson of Bel-nirari and the father of Shalmaneser I. We possess an inscription of his, of which a translation has been given in the first series of the *Records of the Past*, vol. xi. pp. 1-6.
⁶ Agar'sallu is a man's name. The name of the city signifies "Fort of Istar of Agar'sal."   ⁷ *Silim* not *abikta*.
⁸ Literally "divine elder brothers." The "reed of the divine elder brothers" is mentioned in 1266, 5.

28. In regard to a definite boundary, *willingly* (?)¹
29. their boundaries from the direction of the country of PILASQI
30. on the farther² banks of the TIGRIS (and) the city of ARMAN-[AGAR]'SALI
31. as far as (the country) of LULUME they established and fixed.

COLUMN II

Lacuna.

1. his servants he made ......
2. as far as the city of KULLAR ....

3. Bel-kudur-utsur king of ASSYRIA Uras-[pileser]³
4. had slain. Bel-kudur-utsur did Rimmon-[suma-natsir⁴ king of KAR-DUNIAS avenge].
5. With combat (and) slaughter thereupon Uras-pileser [was defeated, and]
6. to his country returned. His many soldiers [did Rimmon-suma-natsir collect, and]
7. marched to the city of ASSUR to capture (it).
8. In the midst of it he fought. He turned about and [returned to his own land].

9. In the time of Zamama-suma-iddin⁵ king of [KAR-DUNIAS]
10. Assur-danan⁶ king of ASSYRIA [marched] against KAR-DU[NIAS].

¹ *Annime.*
² The scribe has written *ammamate* in mistake for *ammate.*
³ It is to Uras-pileser that Tiglath-pileser I. traces his genealogy. He was probably the founder of a dynasty, and his date may perhaps be placed about 1180 B.C.
⁴ For Rimmon-suma-natsir see *Records of the Past*, new series, p. 16, No. 24. ⁵ Or Zamama-nadin-sumi, see vol. i. p. 16, note 5.
⁶ We should probably read Assur-da'an, since the chronological position occupied by the king shows that he must be Assur-da'an the son of Uras-pileser and great-grandfather of Tiglath-pileser I.

11. The cities of ZABAN, IRRIYA (and) AGAR'SAL [he captured].
12. [Their spoil] in abundance [he carried away] to ASSYRIA.[1]

Lacuna.

1. ... to his own country [Assur-ris-ilim][2] returned. After him Nebo-[kudur-utsur king of KAR-DUNIAS]
2. carried his war-engines. To the passes on the frontier of the land of [ASSYRIA]
3. to conquer he went. Assur-ris-ilim king of ASSYRIA
4. mustered his chariots to march against him.
5. Nebo-kudur-utsur, because his engines could not advance, burned his baggage[3] with fire;
6. he turned about and returned to his own country.
7. Nebo-kudur-utsur again (with) a chariot and grooms to the edge of the frontier
8. of ASSYRIA marched to conquer. Assur-ris-ilim
9. sent chariots (and) grooms for defence.[4]
10. He fought with him; he utterly overthrew him; his soldiers he slew;
11. his camp he spoiled, after they had brought back forty of his chariots (with their) coverings.
12. They had taken a standard[5] which went before his host.

13. Tiglath-pileser[6] king of ASSYRIA smote Merodach-nadin-akhi king of KAR-DUNIAS
14. a second time (with) a squadron of chariots, as many as over against the city of ZABAN

[1] These twelve lines come from a fragment belonging to a duplicate copy of the text. [2] The father of Tiglath-pileser I.
[3] Or "ringed encampment." [4] Literally "aid."
[5] Not a proper name Karastu.
[6] Tiglath-pileser I. According to Sennacherib Merodach-nadin-akhi invaded Assyria in the reign of Tiglath-pileser, 418 years before his own capture of Babylon, and consequently 1106 B.C. If the war between Assyria and Babylonia had been provoked by this invasion the accession of Tiglath-pileser would fall 1107 B.C.

15. (on) the Lower (ZAB) in the direction of the city of ARZUKHINA he made,
16. in the second year, on the shore of the sea which is above the land of ACCAD.
17. The cities of DUR-KURIGALZU,[1] SIPPARA of SAMAS,
18. SIPPARA of ANUNIT,[2]
19. BABYLON (and) UPE,[3] great strongholds,
20. together with their fortresses, he captured.
21. At that time the city of AGAR'SAL
22. together with the city of LUBDI he devastated.[4]
23. The country of the SHUHITES[5] as far as the city of RAPIQI, throughout its whole extent, [he conquered].

24. In the time of Assur-bil-kala[6] king [of ASSYRIA, he and]
25. Merodach-sapik-kullat king of KAR-DU[NIAS],
26. friendship[7] (and) complete alliance
27. with one another made.
28. In the time of Assur-bil-kala king of [ASSYRIA]
29. Merodach-sapik-kullat was over[come] by death.
30. Rimmon-bal-iddina the son[8] of Ê-Saggil-saduni the son of a plebeian
31. they raised to the sovereignty over them.
32. [Assur-]bil-kala king of ASSYRIA
33. took (to wife) the daughter of Rimmon-bal-iddina king of KAR-DUNIAS.
34. Her large dowry he brought to ASSYRIA.
35. The men of ASSYRIA (and) of KAR-DUNIAS
36. [lived at peace] with one another.

[1] Now Akerkuf near Bagdad.
[2] Sippara was divided into two quarters, one dedicated to the goddess Anunit, the other (now represented by the mounds of Abu-Habba) to Samas the Sun-god. The double nature of the city has caused it to be called in scripture Sepharvaim "the two Sipparas" (2 Kings xvii. 31).
[3] Upe was at the junction of the Tigris and the Adhem, and was known to classical geographers as Opis. [4] *Ikh*[*liq*].
[5] The Shuhite tribes to which Bildad the friend of Job belonged extended along the western side of the Euphrates northward to the mouth of the Khabour. [6] Assur-bil-kala was the son of Tiglath-pileser I.
[7] Literally "goodness."
[8] The word *abil* is not omitted in the original as is stated by Prof. Tiele.

REVERSE

COLUMN III

1. In the time of Rimmon-nirari[1] king of ASSYRIA, (he and)
2. Samas-suma-damiq king of KAR-DUNIAS
3. set their forces in battle array at the foot of mount YALMAN.
4. Rimmon-nirari king of ASSYRIA overthrew Samas-suma-damiq
5. king of KAR-DUNIAS utterly.
6. He shattered his forces:[2] [his] chariots [and horses harnessed]
7. to the yoke [he carried away].
8. Samas-suma-damiq king of [KAR-DUNIAS]
9. did Nebo-suma-iskun [slay].
10. Rimmon-nirari king [of ASSYRIA with] Nebo-suma-iskun
11. king [of KAR-DUNIAS] fought; he utterly overthrew him.
12. [The cities of] BAMBALA (and) KHUDA[DU][3]
13. [and] many [other] cities
14. [he captured, and] their abundant spoil
15. he took [to ASSYRIA].
16. . . . . . . *tsalmati* was overcome by death.
17. . . . . . . concerning their daughter(s) they [spoke] to one another.
18. [Friendship and] complete alliance they [made] with one another.
19. The men of ASSYRIA (and) ACCAD[4] were united[5] with one another.
20. From the Tel[6] of BIT-BARI which is above the city of ZA[BAN]
21. as far as the Tel of Batani[7] and (the Tel) of the city of ZABDANI they fixed the boundary-line.

---

[1] Rimmon-nirari II, who reigned 911-889 B.C.
[2] *Silim* not *abiktu*. [3] Or Bagdadu.
[4] Northern Babylonia. [5] *Ibba*[*nû*].
[6] Or "mound." [7] The name of a man.

HISTORY OF ASSYRIA AND BABYLONIA

22. [In the] time of Shalmaneser [1] king of [ASSYRIA]
23. [and Nebo-]bal-iddina king of KAR-DUNI[AS]
24. friendship (and) complete alliance
25. [with] one another they made. In the time of Shalmaneser king [of ASSYRIA]
26. [Nebo-]bal-iddina king of KAR-DUNIAS was [overcome] by death.
27. Merodach-nadin-sumi sat on the throne of his father.
28. Merodach-bil-u'sate his brother revolted against him.
29. He seized [the city] of [AH]DABAN. The country of ACCAD
30. was disturbed [everywhere]. Shalmaneser king of [ASSYRIA]
31. to the help of Merodach-nadin-[sumi]
32. king of KAR-DUNIAS marched.
33. Merodach-bil-u'sate the king he smote.[2]
34. The rebel soldiers who (were) with him he slew.
35. [In] KUTHA,[3] BABYLON,
36. [and BORSIPPA [4] he offered sacrifice].[5]

Lacuna.

COLUMN IV

1. He besieged him. That city he took. Bahu-akha-iddin [6]
2. together with his goods (and) the treasures of his palace he took to ASSYRIA.
3. The cities of DUR-ILI,[7] SUKHIRU,[8] GANANATE,

---

[1] Shalmaneser II, who reigned 858-823 B.C.
[2] Or "the king self-appointed along with the rebel soldiers," if we read IM-[GI-DA] with Drs. Peiser and Winckler.
[3] Now Tel Ibrahim a little to the east of Babylon. It is called Cuth in the Old Testament (2 Kings xVii. 30).
[4] Borsippa was the suburb of Babylon which contained the great temple whose ruins are now known as the Birs-i-Nimrud.
[5] This is supplied from an inscription of Shalmaneser.
[6] Bahu-akha-iddin must have been the name of a Babylonian king.
[7] Dur-ili ("the fortress of the god") was in southern Babylonia, near the Elamite frontier.
[8] Or Lakhiru.

4. DUR-KISSAT-PAPSUKAL,[1] the house of the harem, (and) the city of the waters of the DHURNAT,
5. the numerous cities of KAR-DUNIAS,
6. together with their fortresses, their gods (and) their abundant spoil,
7. the Great god, the god KHUMKHUMMU, the goddess of BABYLON, the goddess of ACCAD,
8. the god SIMALIYA, the god NERGAL, the goddess ANUNIT, (and) the divine Son of the Temple
9. of the city of MALI he brought away. To the cities of KUTHA, BABYLON,
10. (and) BORSIPPA he went up. Holy sacrifices [in them] he offered.
11. To the KALDI[2] he descended. The tribute of the kings
12. of the land of the KALDI I received.[3] His officers
13. div[ided] the fields of KAR-DUNI[AS].
14. A definite boundary he fixed.

---

15. Rimmon-nirari[4] king of ASSYRIA . . . [the king of KAR-DUNIAS]
16. subdued.[5] Many soldiers
17. in . . . . . .
18. and . . . . . .
19. men (and) spoil to his place he [brought back].
20. The perpetual obligation of a *corn-tax* (?) he imposed upon them.
21. The men of ASSYRIA (and) KAR-DUNIAS [were united] with one another.

---

[1] Or Dur-Papsukal, "the fortress of the god Papsukal." The city stood on an island in the Tigris, and was probably not far from Gananate on the southern side of the Dhurnat or Diyaleh (the Tornadotos of classical antiquity).

[2] The Kaldi inhabited the marshes at the mouths of the Euphrates and Tigris. Under Merodach-baladan they established themselves in Babylonia and became so important a part of the population as to give their name to the whole of it in classical times. Hence the Kasdim of the Old Testament are represented by "Chaldæans" in the Authorised Version.

[3] This is evidently a quotation from the royal annals.

[4] Rimmon-nirari III, who reigned 810-781 B.C. [5] *Ik-nu-us*.

22. A common boundary in perpetuity they established.
23. The future prince who [shall rule] in ACCAD
24. shall observe it, and [the record] of power (and) conquest
25. may he write, and to this monument [may he hearken]
26. perpetually, and that it may not be forgotten may he [who]
27. has possessed the people listen, and . . .
28. may they exalt the power of ASSYRIA unto [future] days.
29. May he who *shall give laws* (?) to SUMER (and) ACCAD [its words]
30. interpret to all the world.

---

31. [The property of Assur-bani-pal] king of ASSYRIA.

INSCRIPTIONS OF SHALMANESER II

TRANSLATED BY THE REV. V. SCHEIL

SHALMANESER, or more correctly Shulmanu-asharidu II, reigned from 860 to 824 B.C. He was the worthy successor of his father Assur-natsir-pal. The number of his years was equal to the number of his wars. His dominion ended by extending westward as far as Lebanon and the Mediterranean, northward over the countries of Ararat, eastward beyond the oriental sea of Nairi, or Lake Urumiyeh, southward to the left bank of the Euphrates as far as Babylon and the whole of Chaldæa.

Of other labours besides wars, history has preserved the memory only of the restoration of the walls of Calah (Layard's *Inscriptions*, 76), and the construction (or attempt at construction) of a temple to the Moon-god Sin at Haran (*W. A. I.*, v. 64, col. ii. 4).

The principal inscriptions of Shalmaneser are those on an obelisk of black marble, on a monolith from Kurkh, and on the bronze gates of the temple of Balawât. They are all now in the British Museum.

The obelisk was found at Kouyunjik. Besides the chief inscription, it has bas-reliefs with epigraphs attached. The text is published in Layard's *Inscriptions*, 87-98. It has been translated by Oppert (in his *Histoire des Empires de Chaldée et d'Assyrie*), Ménant (*Annales des Rois d'Assyrie*), Sayce (*Records of the Past*, v. 1st series), and Winckler (*Keilinschriftliche Bibliothek*, i.)

The monolith comes from Kurkh. The text has been published in *W.A.I.*, iii. 7, 8, and has been translated by Sayce (*Records of the Past*, iii. 1st series), Ménant (*Annales*), Craig (*Hebraica*, iii. 1887), and Peiser (*Keilinschriftliche Bibliothek*, i.)

The inscription on the gates of Balawât was discovered by Mr. Hormuzd Rassam in 1877, and has been published and translated by Mr. Pinches in the *Transactions of the Society of Biblical Archæology*, vii. pp. 83 *sqq.*

A complete edition of the inscriptions of Shalmaneser II has been published by Amiaud and Scheil. It serves as the basis of the following translations.

INSCRIPTION ON THE OBELISK OF SHALMANESER II

Face A, Top

1. Assur, the great lord, the king of all
2. the great gods; Anu the king of the Igigi
3. and the Anunnaki;[1] the lord of the world, the supreme, Bel
4. the father of the gods, the creator
5. of the universe; Ea, the king of the abyss who determines destinies;
6. Sin, the king of the (lunar) disk, who sheds the light;
7. Adad,[2] the very mighty, the master of abundance; Shamash,
8. the judge of heaven and earth, the ordainer of all things;
9. Merodach, the herald of the gods, the master of the laws; Adar,[3] the captain
10. of the Igigi and the Anunnaki, the god all-powerful; Nergal,
11. the valiant, the king of battles; Nusku who bears the august sceptre,
12. the omniscient god; Beltis, the wife of Bel, the mother of the great gods;
13. Ishtar, the princess of heaven and earth, accomplished in courageous decisions;
14. the great gods who have determined my destinies and enlarged my royalty!
15. Shalmaneser, the king of the multitude of men, high-priest of Assur, the powerful king,

---

[1] That is to say, of the spirits of heaven and earth.
[2] [Ramman, Rimmon.—Ed.]   [3] [Or Uras.—Ed.]

16. the king of all the four regions, the Sun-god of the multitude of mankind, who governs
17. in all countries; the son of Assur-natsir-pal, the supreme priest, whose priesthood unto the gods
18. was pleasing, and who has subdued unto his feet all lands;

FACE B, TOP

19. the illustrious offspring of Tukulti-Adar [1]
20. who subjugated all his enemies and
21. swept them like the tempest.—
22. At the beginning of my reign, when on the throne
23. of the kingdom I had seated myself in state, my chariots
24. (and) my armies I assembled. Into the defiles of the land of SIMESI [2]
25. I penetrated. ARIDU, the strong city
26. of Ninni I captured.—In the first year of my reign
27. I crossed the EUPHRATES in its flood; towards the sea of the setting sun
28. I marched. I purified my weapons in the sea. Victims
29. to my gods I sacrificed. I ascended mount AMANUS; [3]
30. I cut logs of cedar and thuya.
31. I climbed mount LALLAR and erected there an image of my royalty.—
32. In the second year of my reign I approached the city of TIL-BARSAIP.[4] The cities
33. of Akhuni the son of Adini I captured; I shut him up in his city.[5] The EUPHRATES
34. I crossed in its flood. DABIGU, a fortress of the land of the HITTITES,[6]
35. together with the cities that were dependent upon it I captured.—In the third year of my reign Akhuni

---

[1] Tiglath-Uras.
[2] [For the situation of 'Sime'si, see note on line 190.—ED.]
[3] Khamanu.
[4] [Probably the Barsampsê of Ptolemy, though Delitzsch identifies it with Birejik.]   [5] Bit-Adin or Til-Barsip.
[6] [Or "the city Dabigu (and) the city Birtu of the land of the Hittites" (Khatti).—ED.]

36. the son of Adini trembled before my powerful arms, and TIL-BARSAIP,

FACE C, TOP

37. his royal city, he abandoned, and he crossed the EUPHRATES.
38. The city of ANA-ASSUR-UTIR-ATSBAT,[1] situated on the further side
39. of the EUPHRATES, upon the river SAGURRA,[2] which the people
40. of the land of the HITTITES call PITRU,[3]
41. I took for myself. On my return
42. I penetrated into the defiles of the country of ALZI.[4] The countries of ALZI, LUKH[ME],
43. DAYENI (and) NUMME, the city of ARZASHKUN the capital
44. of Arame of the country of URARDHU,[5] the countries of GUZAN (and) KHUPUSHKIA [I have conquered].
45. In the eponymy of Dayan-Assur[6] I departed from NINEVEH; the EUPHRATES
46. I crossed at its flood. I marched against Akhuni the son of Adini; the country of Shitamrat,[7]
47. a mountain peak on the bank of the EUPHRATES, he made his stronghold. The peak
48. of the mountain I assaulted and captured. Akhuni with his gods, his chariots,
49. his horses, his sons, his daughters, (and) his army I carried away and to my city of ASSUR
50. I brought. In that same year I crossed mount KULLAR; to the country of ZAMUA
51. of BITANI[8] I descended. The cities of Nikdiara the prince of the IDIANS

[1] ["For Assur I have taken (it) again"; the name given by Shalmaneser to Pethor.—ED.]   [2] The modern Sajur.
[3] [The Pethor of the Old Testament, to which Balaam belonged.—ED.]
[4] For Alzi, at the sources of the Sebbeneh Su, see *Records of the Past*, new series, i. p. 94, note 4.   [5] Ararat.
[6] [B.C. 854. This was at the beginning of the fifth year of the king's reign.—ED.]   [7] [Or Siparrat.—ED.]
[8] [In Armenia, on the southern shores of Lake Van, so called to distinguish it from another Zamua in Kurdistan between Sulamaniyeh and

52. (and) of Nikdima I captured.—In the fifth year of my reign I ascended mount KASHYARI.[1] Eleven strong cities
53. I captured. I besieged ANKHITTI[2] of the country of the RURIANS in his city. His tribute
54. abundant I received.—In the sixth year of my reign to the cities on the banks of the BALIKHI[3]

FACE D, TOP

55. I approached. They had slain Giammu their governor.
56. I entered the city of TIL-TURAKHE.[4]
57. I crossed the EUPHRATES at its flood.
58. The tribute of the kings of the country of the HITTITES
59. all of them I received. Then Dadda-Idri[5]
60. the king of the country of EMERISHU,[6] Irkhulina[7] of the country of the HAMATHITES, together with the kings
61. of the country of the HITTITES and of the coast of the Sea, to their allied forces
62. trusted, and to offer combat and battle
63. came against me. By the command of ASSUR the great lord, my lord,
64. I fought with them, I defeated them.
65. I took from them their chariots, their litters (?) (and) their war material.

the Shirwan. The Lake of Van is called "the sea of Zamua of Bitani." The Armenian Zamua is also termed Mazamua. *Bitâni* in Assyrian signified "palace," but when applied to Armenia it seems to be intended for an incorrect representation of the native name Biaina(s) or Van.—ED.]   [1] [Mount Masius.—ED.]

[2] [Or perhaps, Ilu-Khitti, see *Records of the Past*, new series, ii. p. 148, note 2.—ED.]

[3] [The modern Belikh, which flows into the Euphrates north of the Khabour.—ED.]

[4] [Perhaps Tiele is right in reading Til-Balakhe, "the mound of Belikh."—ED.]

[5] [Hadad-ezer, which in Aramaic would be Hadad-eder. He is the Ben-hadad of the Old Testament, Ben-Hadad "the son of Hadad," being, as we learn from the cuneiform inscriptions, the name or title of one of the Syrian gods.—ED.]

[6] [The Assyrian name of the kingdom of Damascus, possibly connected with the word Amorite.—ED.]

[7] ["The moon is our god."—ED.]

66. I slew 20,500 of their soldiers with weapons.—
67. In the 7th year of my reign I marched against the cities of Khabini (prince) of TIL-ABNÊ.
68. I captured TIL-ABNÊ his stronghold and the cities dependent on it.
69. I marched to the sources of the TIGRIS, the place from whence the waters gush forth;
70. there I purified the arms of ASSUR; I sacrificed victims to my gods; a feast of rejoicing
71. I made. I erected a great image of my royal majesty. The glory of ASSUR my lord, the exploits
72. of my valour, and all that I had done in these countries, I inscribed upon it; I set (it) up there.—

FACE A, BASE

73. In the 8th year of my reign (against) Merodach-shum-iddin the king of the country of KARDUNIASH[1]
74. Merodach-bel-usate his younger brother revolted. (The country)
75. they divided between them. To avenge
76. Merodach-shum-iddin I marched. I captured the city of ME-TURNAT.[2]—
77. In the 9th year of my reign for the second time I marched to the country of ACCAD.[3]
78. I besieged GANANATE. As for Merodach-bel-usate, the terror
79. of the glory of ASSUR (and) MERODACH overwhelmed him, and to save his life
80. he ascended the mountain. I marched after him. Merodach-bel-usate (and) the soldiers,
81. the rebel-chiefs who were with him I slew with my weapons. To the great cities
82. I marched; I offered sacrifices in BABYLON, BORSIPPA and KUTA.[4]

---

[1] Babylonia.
[2] "The waters of the Turnat" or Tornadotus, the modern Dijâlah, which falls into the Tigris a little below Bagdad. With the name of the city compare that of the capital of Ammon, 2 Sam. xii. 27.
[3] Northern Babylonia.   [4] Now Tell-Ibrahim, east of Babylon.

83. I made offerings to the great gods. I descended to the country of CHALDÆA;[1] I captured their cities.
84. I received the tribute of the kings of the country of CHALDÆA. The *torrent* (?) of my arms overwhelmed as far as the Salt-marshes.[2]—
85. In the 10th year of my reign for the eighth time I crossed the EUPHRATES; I captured the cities of Sangara of CARCHEMISH;[3]
86. I approached the cities of Arame. I captured ARNÊ his royal city and 100 of his towns.—
87. In the 11th year of my reign for the ninth time I crossed the EUPHRATES. I captured cities without number. To the cities of the land of the HITTITES
88. (and) of the country of the HAMATHITES I descended. I captured 89 towns. Dadda-idri of the country of DAMASCUS (and) twelve kings of the country of the HITTITES[4]
89. ranged themselves side by side; I overthrew them.—In the 12th year of my reign for the tenth time I crossed the EUPHRATES.
90. I marched against the country of PAQARKHUBUNA; I carried away their spoil.—In the 13th year of my reign I went up against the country of YAETI;
91. I carried away their spoil.—In the 14th year of my reign I assembled (the men) of the country; I crossed the EUPHRATES; twelve kings met me;
92. I fought [with them]; I overthrew them.—In the 15th year of my reign I marched to the sources of the TIGRIS (and) EUPHRATES. An image
93. I erected in their caverns.—In the 16th year of my reign I crossed the ZAB;[5] to the country of NAMRI[6]

---

[1] *Kaldi*, in the marshes at the head of the Persian Gulf.
[2] Literally "the bitter (river)," *Marrati*: cf. the Merathaim of Jer. l. 21.
[3] [*Gargamis*, now Jerablûs, on the western bank of the Euphrates, a little to the north of the Sajur.—ED.]
[4] [The name is here extended so as to include Syria, Palestine, and even northern Arabia.—ED.]
[5] [Here written *Me-Zaba*, "the water of the (Lower) Zab."—ED.]
[6] [In the Kurdish mountains north of Holwân.—ED.]

94. I marched. Merodach-mudammiq king of NAMRI, to save his life, ascended (the mountain): his goods,
95. his troops (and) his gods I transported to ASSYRIA. Yanzu[1] the son of Khanban I raised to the sovereignty over them.—

FACE B, BASE

96. In the 17th year of my reign I crossed the EUPHRATES; I ascended mount AMANUS; logs
97. of cedar I cut.—In the 18th year of my reign for the sixteenth time I crossed the EUPHRATES. Hazael
98. of the country of DAMASCUS advanced to battle: 1121 chariots, 470 *litters* (?) with
99. his camp I took from him.[2]—In the 19th year of my reign for the eighteenth time I crossed the EUPHRATES. Mount AMANUS
100. I ascended: logs of cedar I cut.—In the 20th year of my reign, for the twentieth time, the EUPHRATES
101. I crossed. Into the country of QAUE[3] I descended. I captured their cities. Their spoil
102. I carried away.—In the 21st year of my reign for the

---

[1] [In the Kassite language, spoken in the district adjoining Namri, *yanzi* signified "king."—ED.]

[2] [The following fragment (*W. A. I.*, iii. 5, No. 6) gives an account of this campaign in further detail:—"In the 18th year of my reign for the 16th time I crossed the EUPHRATES. Hazael of DAMASCUS trusted to the strength of his armies and assembled his armies to a large number. SANIRU (the Biblical Shenir, Deut. iii. 9), a mountain summit as you come to LEBANON, he made his stronghold. I fought with him, I defeated him: 6000 of his soldiers I slew with weapons, 1121 of his chariots, 470 of his war-horses along with his camp I took from him. To save his life he ascended (the mountain). I pursued after him. In DAMASCUS his royal city I shut him up. His plantations I cut down. As far as the mountains of the HAURAN I marched. The cities to a countless number I threw down, dug up (and) burned with fire. Their spoil to a countless amount I carried away. As far as the mountain of BAHLI-RAHSI (Baal-rosh at the mouth of the Dog River), which (is) a headland of the sea, I marched: an image of my majesty I set up upon it. At that time I received the tribute of the TYRIANS, the SIDONIANS (and) of Yahua (Jehu) the son of Khumrí (Omri)."—ED.]

[3] [Elsewhere written Que. They seem to have inhabited the northern shore of the Gulf of Antioch. Lenormant has suggested that the name occurs in 1 Kings x. 28, where the word translated "linen yarn" ought to be rendered "from Queh."—ED.]

21st time I crossed the EUPHRATES. Against the cities
103. of Hazael of the country of DAMASCUS I marched; four of his cities I captured. The tribute of the TYRIANS,
104. the SIDONIANS (and) the GEBALITES[1] I received.—In the 22d year of my reign for the 22d time the EUPHRATES
105. I crossed. I descended into the country of TUBAL.[2] At that time from the twenty-four
106. kings of TUBAL I received gifts. To mount TUMAR,
107. a mountain of silver, a mountain of *muli*,[3] a mountain of marble, I marched.—In the 23d year of my reign
108. the EUPHRATES I crossed. UETASH the stronghold
109. of Lalla the MILIDIAN[4] I captured. The kings of TUBAL
110. had come; their tribute I received.—In the 24th year of my reign the Lower ZAB
111. I crossed. I passed over mount KHASHIMUR; into the country of NAMRI
112. I descended. Yanzû the king of NAMRI before
113. my powerful weapons trembled, and to save his life
114. ascended (the mountain). SIKHISHALAKH, BIT-TAMUL, BIT-SAKKI
115. (and) BIT-SHÊDI his strong cities I captured. His soldiers I slew.
116. His spoil I carried away. I threw down, dug up (and) burned with fire the cities.
117. The survivors of them ascended the mountains. The mountain peaks
118. I assaulted, I captured: their soldiers I slew; their spoil (and) their goods

[1] See Josh. xiii. 5; 1 Kings v. 32; Ez. xxvii. 9. Gebal was the classical Byblos, eight miles north of Beyrout.
[2] [*Tabali*, the Tibareni of classical geography. In the Assyrian period they lived between the Muskâ or Meshech and Komagênê, to the east of Malatiyeh.—ED.]
[3] [Perhaps "salt."—ED.]
[4] Milid is represented by the modern Malatiyeh.

119. I carried down. I departed from the country of NAMRI. The tribute of twenty-seven kings
120. of the country of PARSUA[1] I received. From PARSUA I departed. Into
121. the country of MESSI, the country of the AMADIANS,[2] the country of ARAZIASH (and) the country of KHARKHAR I descended.

FACE C, BASE

122. The cities of KUAKINDA, KHATSTSANABI,[3] ESAMUL
123. (and) KINABLILA as well as the towns dependent on them I captured. Their soldiers
124. I slew, their spoil I carried away. The cities I threw down, dug up (and) burned with fire. An image of my majesty
125. in the country of KHARKHÂRA I set up. Yanzû the son of Khaban, with his numerous goods,
126. his gods, his sons, his daughters (and) his many troops I carried away, to ASSYRIA I brought (them).—In the 25th year of my reign
127. the EUPHRATES at its flood I crossed. I received the tribute of all the kings of the country of the HITTITES. Mount AMANUS
128. I passed over. I descended into the cities of Katê of the country of the QAUIANS. TIMUR his stronghold
129. I assaulted, I captured. I slew their soldiers. I carried away their spoil. The cities to a countless number I threw down, dug up
130. (and) burned with fire. On my return MÛRU the stronghold of Arame the son of Agusi
131. I took for myself as a fortress.[4] I surrounded its enclosure (with a wall); I founded therein a palace as my royal abode.—
132. In the 26th year of my reign for the 7th time I passed

---

[1] [Also called Par'suas; in the Vannic inscriptions Bar'suas. It lay to the south-east of the Mannâ or Minni on the south-western shore of Lake Urumiyeh.—ED.]
[2] [*Amadâ*, probably to be identified with Madâ or "Medes." If so, this is the earliest mention we have of the latter people.—ED.]
[3] [Or Tarzanabi.—ED.]   [4] *Birtu.*

over Mount AMANUS; for the 4th time against the cities of Katê

133. of the country of the QAUIANS I marched. I besieged TANAKUN[1] the stronghold of Tulka. The terror
134. of the glory of ASSUR my lord overwhelmed him and they came forth, they took my feet. I took hostages from him. Silver, gold,
135. iron, oxen (and) sheep I received from him as his tribute. I departed from TANAKUN; against the country of LAMENA
136. I marched. The inhabitants fled; they occupied an inaccessible mountain; the summit of the mountain I assaulted,
137. I captured. Their soldiers I slew; their spoil, their oxen (and) their sheep I brought down from the mountain.
138. I threw down, dug up (and) burned with fire their cities. Against the city of TARZI[2] I marched. They took my feet. Silver (and) gold,
139. I received as their tribute. Kirrî the brother of Katê to the sovereignty over them
140. I appointed. On my return I ascended over mount AMANUS. Logs of cedar I cut,
141. I removed, to my city of ASSUR I transported.—In the 27th year of my reign I assembled my chariots (and) my armies. Dayân-Assur
142. the Tartan,[3] the commander of my numerous armies, at the head of my troops against the country of ARARAT I despatched,
143. I sent. Into the country of BIT-ZAMANI[4] he descended; into the defiles of the city of AMMASH he entered; the river ARZANIA[5] he crossed.

---

[1] [Compare the name of Thanakê given by Apollodoros (iii. 14, 3, 1) as the wife of Sandakos, who came from Syria to Kilikia and there founded Kelenderis; she was the mother of Kinyras and the daughter of king Megessaros.—ED.] [2] Tarsus.
[3] [*Turtannu* or "commander-in-chief." See Is. xx. 1; 2 Kings xviii. 17.—ED.] [4] [Literally "the house of the country of Zamani."—ED.]
[5] [The Arsanias of classical geography, which joins the Euphrates near Mush to the west of Lake Van.—ED.]

144. Seduri[1] of the country of the ARARATIANS heard and to the strength of his numerous armies
145. trusted; he came against [2] me to make combat (and) battle. I[2] fought with him,
146. I defeated him; I filled the wide plain with the bodies of his warriors.—In the 28th year of my reign,
147. while I was staying in CALAH, news was brought to me (that) the men of the country of the PATINIANS[3]
148. had slain Lubarni their prince (and) had raised to the sovereignty over them Surri who had no right to the throne.
149. Dayan-Assur the Tartan, the commander of my numerous armies, at the head of my army (and) my train
150. I despatched, I sent. He crossed the EUPHRATES at its flood. In KINALUA,[4] the royal city of (Surri),
151. he made a massacre. As for Surri the usurper, the terror of the glory of ASSUR my lord
152. overwhelmed him and he died a natural death. The men of the country of the PATINIANS before the splendour of my powerful weapons

FACE D, BASE

153. trembled, and they seized the sons of Surri and the leaders in the rebellion (and) delivered (them) to me.
154. I hung these men on gibbets. Sasi a son of the country of UTSTSÂ took my feet; to the sovereignty

---

[1] [Sarduris I., of the native Vannic texts, of whom we have two inscriptions in the Assyrian language, both found at Van. He introduced the cuneiform system of writing into Armenia, and seems to have founded the Vannic kingdom. In his inscriptions he calls himself the son of Lutipris and king of Nairi, and claims to have built the citadel of Van. His son and successor, Isbuinis, substituted the native language for Assyrian in his inscriptions. See my Memoir on the *Cuneiform Inscriptions of Van*, Jrl. R. A. S., xiv. 3, 4; xx. 1.—ED.]

[2] Shalmaneser here identifies himself with his commander-in-chief.

[3] [The Patinâ inhabited the district between the eastern bank of the Afrin and the Gulf of Antioch, extending southward to the Orontes.—ED.]

[4] [Also called Kunulua and Kinalia, between the Afrin and the Orontes, perhaps the classical Gindarus.—ED.]

155. over them I appointed (him). I received from them silver, gold, lead, copper, iron, (and) ivory to a countless amount.
156. I made a very lofty image of my majesty; I placed (it) in KINALUA his royal city in the house of his gods.—In the 29th
157. year of my reign my armies (and) train I despatched, I sent. I ascended to the country of KIRKHI.[1] Their cities I threw down,
158. dug up (and) burned with fire. Their country I swept like the tempest. The terror
159. of my glory I poured over them.—In the 30th year of my reign, while I was staying in CALAH, Dayan-Assur
160. the Tartan, the commander of my numerous armies, I despatched, I sent at the head of my armies. The ZAB
161. he crossed, he made his way to the cities of KHUBUSHKÂ.[2] The tribute of Datana
162. the KHUBUSHKIAN I received. From the cities of the KHUBUSHKIAN
163. I departed. He[3] approached the cities of Makdubi[4] the MALKHISIAN. Tribute
164. I received. He[3] departed from the cities of the MALKHISIANS. To the cities of Ualki
165. the MANNIAN[5] he approached. Ualki the MANNIAN before the splendour of my puissant weapons
166. trembled, and quitted ZIRTA his royal city, and to save his life ascended (the mountains).
167. I pursued after him; I brought back his oxen, his

---

[1] [Probably the same as Qurkhi "opposite the land of the Hittites." See *Records of the Past*, new series, ii. p. 140, note 4.—ED.]
[2] [Khubuska, also called Khubuskia, lay on the north-eastern frontier of Assyria, between the Zab and the territory of the Minni.—ED.]
[3] That is to say Dayan-Assur.
[4] [Or Maggubbi.—ED.]
[5] [The Manná, called the Manâ in the Vannic inscriptions, are the Minni of Old Testament (Jer. l. 27), who inhabited the country on the eastern border of the kingdom of Ararat or Van, and extended along the western shore of Lake Urumiyeh.—ED.]

sheep (and) his goods to a countless number. His cities

168. I threw down, dug up (and) burned with fire. He[1] departed from the country of the MANNÂ; to the cities of Shulusunu of the country of KHARRU

169. he approached. He captured MASASHURU his royal city as well as the cities dependent on it. To Shulusunu

170. and his sons I granted pardon. I restored him to his country. Gifts (and) tribute, horses trained

171. to the yoke I imposed upon him. He approached SHURDIRA. The tribute of Artasari

172. the SHURDIRIAN I received. Into the country of PARSUA[2] I descended. The tribute of the kings

173. of the country of PARSUA I received. As for the rest of the country of PARSUA (which was) not obedient to ASSUR, their cities

174. I captured, their spoil (and) their goods I carried away to ASSYRIA.—In the 31st year of my reign, for the second time, the face

175. I *fixed* (?) on ASSUR (and) HADAD.[3] At that time, while I was staying in CALAH, Dayan-Assur

176. the Tartan, the commander of my numerous armies, at the head of my armies (and) my train I despatched, I sent.

177. The cities of DATÂ[4] the KHUBUSHKIAN he approached. Tribute I received.

178. Against the city of TSAPPARIA the stronghold of the country of MUTSATSIRA[5] I marched. The city of TSAPPARIA together with

179. 46 cities of the MUTSATSIRIANS he captured. As far as the fortresses of the people of ARARAT

180. I marched. I threw down, dug up (and) burned with

---

[1] That is to say Dayan-Assur.   [2] See p. 46, note 1, above.
[3] [Or Rimmon.—ED.]   [4] Called Datana above, line 161.
[5] [Mutsatsira lay on the southern border of the kingdom of Ararat or Van, and was destroyed by Sargon in B.C. 714. The cylinder of its last king Urzana is now in the Museum of the Hague. See my Memoir on the Vannic Inscriptions, p. 673.—ED.]

fire their cities. Into the country of GUZAN[1] I descended. The tribute

181. of Ubû the GUZANIAN, of the MANNIANS, the .. BURISIANS, the KHARRANIANS,[2]
182. the SHASHGANIANS, the ANDIANS (and) the A ... RIANS, oxen, sheep, and horses
183. trained to the yoke I received. I descended into the cities of the country of . . . ; the cities of PERRIA
184. (and) SHITIUARYA[3] his cities, with twenty-two towns dependent on it, I threw down, dug up
185. (and) burned with fire. I spread over them the terror of my glory. He marched against the cities of the PARSUANS.
186. The cities of BUSHTU,[4] SHALA-KHAMANU, (and) KINIKHAMANU, strongholds, together with 22 cities
187. which (were) dependent on them I captured. I slew their fighting men, I carried away their spoil. Into the country of NAMRI I descended.
188. The terror of the glory of ASSUR (and) MERODACH overwhelmed them; they abandoned their cities, to
189. inaccessible mountains they ascended. I threw down, dug up (and burned with fire 250 of their cities.
190. I descended through the pass of SIMESI, the key[5] of the country of KHALMAN.

[1] [This northern Guzan or Gozan was different from the Gozan near Diarbekir, at the sources of the Khabour, to which the Israelites were transported according to 2 Kings xviii. 11. See Epigraph I.—ED.]
[2] [Not to be confounded with the famous city of Kharran or Haran in Mesopotamia, mentioned in Genesis.—ED.]
[3] [Called Satiraraus in the Vannic Inscriptions.—ED.]
[4] [Called the country of Bustus in the Vannic inscriptions, from which we learn that it lay to the south-east of the Mannâ. It would have occupied the southern shore of Lake Urumiyeh.—ED.]
[5] [Literally "at the head." Khalman, or rather Khalvan, is the modern Holwan. It was here, at Sir-Pul, that Sir H. Rawlinson discovered the cuneiform inscription of Kannubanini king of the Lulubini.— ED.]

The Epitaphs over the Bas-Reliefs

I

I have received the tribute of Sûa of the country of GUZAN: silver, gold, lead, vases of copper, sceptres for the hand of the king, horses, (and) dromedaries with two humps.

II

I have received the tribute of Jehu, the son of Omri:[1] silver, gold, bowls of gold, chalices of gold, cups of gold, pails of gold, lead, sceptres for the hand of the king, (and) spear-shafts.

III

I have received the tribute of the country of MUTSRI:[2] dromedaries with two humps, an ox of the river SAKEYA (?) an antelope, elephants,[3] (and) apes *with their young* (?)

IV

I have received the tribute of Merodach-abil-utsur of the country of the SHUHITES:[4] silver, gold, pails of gold, ivory, spear-shafts, *bûya*, embroidered vestments, (and) linen.

V

I have received the tribute of Garparunda of the country of the PATINIANS: silver, gold, lead, copper, vases of copper, ivory, (and) boxwood.

---

[1] "Yahua the son of Khumri." This was in B.C. 842. Shalmaneser was misinformed in regard to the relationship of Jehu to the dynasty of Omri. Samaria, however, was known to the Assyrians as "the House of Omri," in consequence of their first becoming acquainted with it in the reign of Ahab.

[2] Mutsri lay to the north-east of Khorsabad on the caravan route from the east. See *Records of the Past*, new series, i. p. 109, note 7.

[3] [Rather "female elephants." Perhaps the next word *basiati* is an adjective in agreement. The "ox" would be either a yak or a rhinoceros according to the bas-relief.—ED.]

[4] [*Sukhâ*. The Shuhites extended along the western bank of the Euphrates from the Khabour to the Belikh. Cf. Job ii. 11.—ED.]

THE MONOLITH INSCRIPTION OF SHALMANESER II

TRANSLATED BY THE REV. V. SCHEIL.

THE inscription of which a translation is here given is engraved on a monolith found at Kurkh, and now in the British Museum. Kurkh, which is probably the Karkathiokerta of classical geography, is upon the right bank of the Tigris, about 20 miles to the south of Diarbekir. The monument was erected to commemorate the exploits of the Assyrian king, Shalmaneser II, during the first four and a half years of his reign (B.C. 858-854). It gives in detail an account of the campaigns which are briefly noticed in the annals of the Black Obelisk.

The inscription has been translated by Ménant in the *Annales des Rois d'Assyrie* (1874), pp. 105-113; by Sayce in the *Records of the Past*, 1st series, iii. pp. 81-100 (1874); by. Craig in *Hebraica*, iii. pp. 201 *sqq.* (1887); and by Peiser in the *Keilinschriftliche Bibliothek*, i. pp. 151-175 (1889). The geographical and historical information contained in it makes it a peculiarly valuable document, especially when studied in connection with the inscription of the Black

Obelisk, and the long standard inscription of Assur-natsir-pal. It contains the first mention found in an Assyrian text of an Israelitish king, and proves that the death of Ahab could not have taken place until after B.C. 854.

THE MONOLITH INSCRIPTION OF SHALMANESER II

COLUMN I

1. ASSUR the great lord, the king of all the great gods; ANU the king of the IGIGI and ANUNNAKI,[1] the master of the world; BEL the father of the gods, who determines destiny,
2. who institutes the laws [of heaven and earth]; EA, the wise, the king of the Abyss, the discoverer of cunning arts; SIN the illuminator of heaven (and) earth, the illustrious god; SHAMASH
3. the judge of the (four) zones, the director of mankind; ISHTAR the lady of battles and combats, whose delight (is) conflict; the great gods who love my royalty,
4. my empire, my power, and my government have they magnified; a famous name, an illustrious renown, above all the sovereigns (of the world) have they bestowed on me in abundance!
5. Shalmaneser, the king of the multitudes of men, the sovereign pontiff of ASSUR, the powerful king, the king of ASSYRIA, the king of all the four zones, the Sun-god[2] of the multitudes of men,
6. who governs all the world; the king who fears the gods, the favourite[3] of BEL, the appointed vicar of ASSUR, the august prince, who has traversed

---

[1] The spirits of heaven and earth.

[2] [The identification of the king with the Sun-god is frequent in the cuneiform tablets of Tel el-Amarna, where it is an imitation of an Egyptian usage. It is probable that the application of the term to the Assyrian king was due to the early influence of Egypt.—ED.]

[3] [Literally " the pupil of the eyes."—ED.]

7. easy paths and difficult roads, who has trodden the summits of the mountains (and) all (their) ranges, who has received tribute and presents
8. from all regions, who has opened the mountains above and below; before the onset of whose mighty battle the regions (of the world) have yielded,
9. the world has trembled to its foundations before his warlike fury; the male hero who has marched under the protection of ASSUR (and) SHAMASH the gods his allies;
10. who has no rival among the kings of the four zones (of the world); the royal despot of the world, who has traversed difficult roads, (and) has advanced over mountains and seas;
11. the son of Assur-natsir-pal, the vicegerent of BEL, the priest of ASSUR, whose priesthood has been pleasing to the gods, and who has subjected to his feet all lands; the illustrious descendant of Tukulti-Adar [1]
12. who subjugated all his foes, and swept them like the tempest, when ASSUR the great lord in the determination of his [heart] had turned upon me his illustrious eyes, and
13. had called me to the government [2] of ASSYRIA; had given me to hold the mighty weapon which overthrows the rebellious; had [invested] me with the [sacred] crown; the lordship over all lands
14. had granted me; had strongly urged me to conquer and subjugate: in those days at the beginning of my reign, in the first of my (regnal) years,[3]
15. (when) I had seated myself in state on the throne of royalty, I summoned my chariots (and) armies; into the defiles of the country of SIMESI I entered; to ARIDU the fortified city
16. of Ninni I approached. The city I besieged, I captured; its numerous soldiers I slew; its spoil I

---

[1] Or Tiglath-Uras.
[2] Literally "had called me as a prophet (*nabium*) to the shepherding."
[3] B.C. 858.

carried away. I erected a pyramid of heads at the entrance of his city.

17. Their youths and maidens I delivered to the flames.[1] While I remained in ARIDU the tribute of the people of KHARGA, KHARMASA,

18. SIMESI, SIMERA, SIRISHA, (and) ULMANIA, horses trained to the yoke, oxen, sheep, (and) wine I received. From ARIDU

19. I departed; difficult paths (and) inaccessible mountains whose peaks rose to the sky like the point of an iron sword I cut with axes of bronze (and) copper. The chariots

20. (and) troops I caused to cross (them). To the city of KHUPUSHKIA I approached. KHUPUSHKIA with 100 towns which (were) dependent on it I burned with fire. Kakia

21. a king of the country of NAIRI and the rest of his troops trembled before the splendour of my arms, and occupied the strong mountains. After them I ascended the mountains,

22. I fought a hard battle in the midst of the mountains (and) utterly destroyed them. I brought back from the mountains chariots, troops, (and) horses trained to the yoke. The terror of the glory

23. of ASSUR my lord overwhelmed them; they descended (and) took my feet. Taxes and tribute I imposed upon them. From the city of KHUPUSHKIA I departed.

24. To SUGUNIA the stronghold of Arame of ARARAT[2] I approached. The city I besieged, I captured; their numerous soldiers I slew.

25. Its spoil I carried away. I erected a pyramid of heads at the entrance of his city; 14 towns which (were) dependent on it I burned with fire. From SUGUNIA

---

[1] [Literally, "I burned for a holocaust." There seems to be a reference to human sacrifice; cf. 2 Kings iii. 27.—ED.]

[2] [In the time of Shalmaneser the kingdom of Ararat, with its capital near Lake Van, was distinguished from Nairi, with its centre at Khubuskia. See *Records of the Past*, new series, i. p. 106, note 7.—ED.]

26. I departed; to the sea of the country of NAIRI[1] I descended. I purified my weapons in the sea; I sacrificed victims to my gods. In those days an image of my person
27. I made; I inscribed upon it the glory of ASSUR the great lord, my lord, and the mightiness of my empire; I erected (it) overlooking the sea. On my return
28. from the sea I received the tribute of Asû of the land of GUZAN in abundance, horses, oxen, sheep, wine, (and) two camels with two humps;
29. to my city of ASSUR I brought (them).—In the month Iyyar, on the 13th day,[2] I departed from NINEVEH. I crossed the TIGRIS. I passed through the mountains[3] of KHASAMU and DIKHNUNU.
30. To LA'LA'TE[4] a city of Akhuni the son of Adini I approached. The terror of the glory of ASSUR my lord overwhelmed [them, to the mountains . . .]
31. they ascended. The city I threw down, dug up (and) burned with fire. From LA'LA'TE I departed. [To KI . . . QA the stronghold]
32. of Akhuni the son of Adini I approached. Akhuni the son of Adini to the multitude [of his troops trusted, and to make] combat and battle [came against] me. Under the protection of ASSUR
33. and the great gods, my lords, I fought with him; I utterly defeated him. I shut him up in his city. From the city of KI . . . QA I departed;
34. to BUR-MAR'ÂNA[5] a city of Akhuni the son of Adini [I approached. The city] I besieged, I captured. I destroyed with my weapons 300 of his fighting-men. A pyramid of heads
35. I erected [at the entrance to his city]. The tribute of

---

[1] Lake Van.
[2] B.C. 857. The eVents of the year are summed up in the annals of the Black Obelisk, lines 26-31.
[3] [Or "countries."— ED.]   [4] [Lahlahte.—ED.]
[5] [Perhaps an Aramaic name signifying " the son of our lord."—ED.]

INSCRIPTIONS OF SHALMANESER II

Khapini[1] of TIL-ABNA,[2] of Ga'uni of SA[LLU], ... of Giri-Dadda [3]

36. [of ASSU], silver, gold, oxen, sheep, (and) wine I received. From the city of BUR-MAR'ÂNA I departed; in boats of seal-skin the EUPHRATES

37. I crossed. The tribute of Qata-zilu of KUMMUKH,[4] silver, gold, oxen, sheep, (and) wine I received. To the city of PAQARRUKHBUNI [5]

38. (and) the cities of Akhuni the son of Adini on the farther bank of the EUPHRATES I approached. I utterly destroyed the country. Its cities to ruins

39. I reduced. I filled the broad plain with the corpses of his warriors; 1300 of his fighting-men I slew with weapons.

40. From the city PAQARRUKHBUNI I departed; to the cities of Mutalli [6] of the city of the GAMGUMIANS I approached. The tribute

41. of Mutalli of the city of the GAMGUMIANS, silver, gold, oxen, sheep, wine, (and) his daughter with a large dowry I received. From the city of GAMGUMÊ

42. I departed; LUTIBU the stronghold of Khânu of the country of the SAM'ALIANS I approached. Khânu of the country of the SAM'ALIANS, Sapalulme [7]

43. of the country of the PATINIANS,[8] Akhuni the son of Adini, Sangara of the country of the CARCHEMISHIANS, trusted to their mutual alliance and prepared for

44. battle; they came against me to fight. By the supreme

---

[1] Called Khabini by Assur-natsir-pal and on the Black Obelisk.
[2] ["The mound of stones."—ED.]
[3] [Or perhaps Ki-giri-Dadda: he is called Giri-Dadi by Assur-natsir-pal, *Records of the Past*, new series, ii. p. 173, note 1.—ED.]
[4] Komagênê.
[5] Called Paqarkhubuna on the Black Obelisk, line 90.
[6] [The name of Mutalli is the same as that of the Hittite king Mutal, formerly read Mautenar, who is mentioned in the Egyptian copy of the treaty concluded between Ramses II, the Egyptian monarch, and the Hittites of Kadesh.—ED.]
[7] [Or Sapa-lulve, the Saplil of the Egyptian texts.—ED.]
[8] Between the Afrin and the gulf of Antioch, extending southwards to the sources of the Orontes.

power of NERGAL who marches before me, with the forceful weapons

45. which ASSUR the lord has granted (me) I fought with them, I utterly defeated them. Their combatants
46. I slew with weapons; like HADAD[1] I poured the deluge upon them, I heaped them up in the ditches; with the bodies
47. of their warriors I filled the broad plain; with their blood I dyed the mountains like wool. (His) many chariots [and troops], (and) horses
48. trained for the yoke I took from him.[2] I erected a pyramid of heads at the entrance to his city. His cities I threw down, dug up (and) burned with fire.
49. In those days I celebrated the greatness of the great gods; I proclaimed for ever the valour of ASSUR and SHAMASH. A great image of my royalty
50. I made; I inscribed upon it the exploits of my valour (and) the deeds of my glory. At the source of the river SALUARA
51. at the foot of mount AMANUS I erected (it). From mount AMANUS I departed; the ORONTES[3] I crossed; to ALIMUSH[4]
52. the stronghold of Sapalulme the PATINIAN I approached. Sapalulme the PATINIAN to save
53. his life [called to his aid] Akhuni the son of Adini, Sangara the CARCHEMISHIAN, Khayânu the SAM'ALIAN, Kate-[zilu the KOMAGENIAN], . . .
54. the QUAN,[5] Pikhirim the CILICIAN,[6] Bur-anate the YASBUKIAN, Ada . . . . . the country of ASSYRIA

COLUMN II

1. . . . . . .
2. . . . I shattered [his forces]; the city I besieged, I captured. . . .
3. . . . his numerous chariots (and) horses trained to the yoke . . . I carried away . . .

---

[1] Rimmon.
[2] That is, Akhuni.
[3] *Arantu.*
[4] Or Alizir.
[5] Twenty-five years later the king of Que was Kate or Kati; see Black Obelisk, line 132.
[6] *Khilukâ.*

4. [His fighting-men] I slew [with] weapons. In the midst of this battle Bur-anate . . . . . .
5. . . . my hands captured. The great cities of the PATINIAN I in[vested. The countries]
6. of the Upper [Sea][1] of SYRIA[2] and of the sea of the setting sun I swept like a mound under a storm.
7. The tribute of the kings of the sea-coast I received. On the shores of the broad sea, straight before me, victoriously
8. I marched. An image of my majesty I made to perpetuate my name for ever, overlooking the sea I e[rected it].
9. To the mountains of AMANUS I ascended. Logs of cedar and thuya I cut. To the mountains
10. of mount ATALUR where the image of Assur-irbi[3] was set up I marched. I erected an image by the side of his image. From the sea I went [down];
11. the cities of TAYÂ . . , KHAZAZU,[4] NULIA (and) BUTÂMU belonging to the PATINIAN I captured; 2800 fighting-men
12. I slew; 14,600 prisoners I carried away. The tribute of Arame the son of Gusi,[5] silver, gold, oxen,
13. sheep, wine, (and) couches of gold and silver I received. —In the year of my own eponymy,[6] on the 13th day of the month Iyyar from [NINEVEH]
14. I departed; the TIGRIS I crossed, the mountains[7] of KHASAMU and DIKHNUNU I traversed. To TIL-BURSIP[8] the stronghold of Akhuni
15. the son of Adini I approached. Akhuni the son of

---

[1] The Mediterranean. [2] Literally, "the country of the west."
[3] [The Assyrian king Assur-irbi is otherwise unknown, but he probably reigned in the interval between Samsi-Rimmon I, B.C. 1070, and Tiglath-pileser II, B.C. 950. For his identification with Assur-rab-buri, see note on line 37.—ED.]
[4] [The modern 'Azaz, about twenty-two miles north-west of Aleppo. —ED.] .
[5] [Called Agûsi in line 27, and on the Black Obelisk.—ED.]
[6] B.C. 856; Black Obelisk, lines 32-35. [7] Or countries.
[8] [Probably meaning in Aramaic "Mound of the Son of 'Sip," a name which must be identified with that of Saph in 2 Sam. xxi. 18. Til-Bur'sip is also written Til-Bur'saip and Til-Bar'sip.—ED.]

Adini trusted to the multitude of his troops and came to meet me. I utterly defeated him. In [his city]

16. I shut him up. From TIL-BURSIP I departed; in boats of seal-skin the EUPHRATES at its flood I crossed. AL (?) ... GÂ, TAGI ...,

17. SÛRUNU, PARIPA, TIL-BASHERÊ[1] (and) DABIGU, six strongholds of Akhuni the son of Adini I [besieged], I captured. His numerous fighting-men

18. I slew: their spoil I carried away; 200 towns which (were) dependent on them I threw down, dug up (and) burned with fire. [From] DABIGU I (departed);

19. to SAZABÊ the stronghold of Sangara the CARCHE-MISHIAN I approached. The city I besieged, I captured. Their numerous fighting-men I slew;

20. their spoil I carried away. The towns which (were) dependent on him I threw down, dug up (and) burned with fire. The kings of the country [of the HITTITES] all of them,

21. trembled before the splendour of my powerful weapons and my violent onset, and they took my feet. From . . . shun[2] the PATINIAN

22. 3 talents of gold, 100 talents of silver, 300 talents of copper, 300 talents of iron, 1000 vases of copper, 1000 vestments of embroidered stuff (and) linen, his daughter

23. with her abundant dowry, 20 talents of blue purple, 500 oxen, (and) 5000 sheep, I received. A talent of gold, 2 talents of blue purple, (and) 100 logs of cedar

24. I imposed upon him as tribute; each year I receive (it) in my city of ASSUR. From Khayânu the son

---

[1] [Probably the modern Tel Basher; see *Records of the Past*, new series, i. p. 109, note 5, and ii. p. 166, note 3. The printed text of the inscription has to be corrected here.—ED.]

[2] [This king must have been the successor of Sapalulve mentioned in Column I, and the predecessor of Girparuda mentioned in Column II, line 84.—ED.]

of Gabbaru who (dwells) at the foot of mount AMANUS 10 talents of silver, 90 talents

25. of copper, 30 talents of iron, 300 vestments of embroidered stuff (and) linen, 300 oxen, 3000 sheep, 200 logs of cedar . . . 2 *homers* of cedar-resin

26. (and) his daughter with her dowry I received. I laid upon him as tribute 10 manehs of silver, 200 logs of cedar, (and) a *homer* of cedar-resin ; each year

27. I receive (it). From Aramu the son of Agûsi 10 manehs of gold, 6 talents of silver, 500 oxen, (and) 5000 sheep I received. From Sangara the CARCHEMISHIAN 2 talents

28. of gold, 70 talents of silver, 30 talents of copper, 100 talents of iron, 20 talents of blue purple, 500 weapons, his daughter with a dowry, and 100 daughters of his nobles,

29. 500 oxen, (and) 5000 sheep, I received. I laid upon him as tribute a maneh of gold, a talent of silver, (and) 2 talents of blue purple ; each year I receive (it). From Qata-zilu

30. the KOMAGENIAN I receive each year 20 manehs of silver (and) 300 logs of cedar.—In the eponymy of Assur-bel-kain,[1] on the 13th day of the month Tammuz, I departed from NINEVEH ;

31. the TIGRIS I crossed ; the mountains of KHASAMU and DIKHNUNU I traversed. At TIL-BARSIP the stronghold of Akhuni the son of Adini I arrived. Akhuni

32. the son of Adini, before the splendour of my powerful weapons and my violent onset, to save his life, crossed [to the western bank] of the EUPHRATES ;

33. to other countries he passed over. By the command of ASSUR the great lord, my lord, the cities of TIL-BARSIP (and) ALIGU [I occupied. The city of] . . . SHAGUQA as my royal city

34. I chose. I settled men of ASSYRIA within (it). I founded palaces within it for the habitation of my

---

[1] B.C. 856. Black Obelisk, lines 35 *sq.*

majesty. To TIL-BARSIP the name of KAR-SHALMANESER,[1]

35. to NAPPIGU the name of LITA-ASSUR,[2] to ALIGU the name of ATSBAT-LA-KUNU,[3] to RUGULITI the name of QIBIT-[ASSUR][4] I gave. In those days

36. the city of ANA-ASSUR-UTIR-ATSBAT,[5] which the HITTITES call PITRU,[6] which (is) upon the river SAGURA on the farther side of the EUPHRATES,

37. and the city of MUTKÎNU which is upon the hither side of the EUPHRATES, which Tiglath-Pileser,[7] the royal forefather who went before me had [captured] (and which) in the time of Assur-Irbi (?),[8]

38. the king of ASSYRIA, the king of the country of ARAM[9] had taken away by force, these cities I restored to their (former) position, I settled men of ASSYRIA in them.

39. While I was staying in the city of KAR-SHALMANESER the tribute of the kings of the sea-coast and of the kings of the banks of EUPHRATES, silver, gold, lead, copper,

40. vases of copper, oxen, sheep, (and) embroidered and linen vestments I received. From KAR-SHALMANESER I departed; mount [10] SUMU I traversed.

41. Into the country of BIT-ZAMÂNI I descended. From BIT-ZAMÂNI I departed; the mountains[11] of NAMDÂNU (and) MERKHISU I traversed. Difficult paths (and) mountains

42. inaccessible whose peaks rose to the sky like the point

---

[1] "The Fortress of Shalmaneser."   [2] "The Glory of Assur."
[3] "I have taken; (it is) not yours."   [4] "The Command of Assur."
[5] "To Assur I have restored, I have taken."
[6] [The Pethor of the Old Testament, from which Balaam came. We learn from this and parallel passages that it stood on the eastern side of the Sagura, the modern Sajur, not far from the junction of this river with the Euphrates.—ED.]
[7] [Tiglath-pileser I, B.C. 1100. The name may be a modified form of that of Mitanni, for which see *Records of the Past*, new series, i. p. 113.—ED.]
[8] [The reading of the name is doubtful, the characters being partly obliterated. George Smith read Assur-rab-buri.—ED].   [9] *Arumu.*
[10] Or "country of Sumu."   [11] Or "countries."

of a sword I cut with axes of bronze. I caused chariots (and) troops to pass (them). Into the country of ENZITE[1] in mount SHUA[2]
43. I descended. My hand conquered the country of ENZITE throughout its extent. Their cities I threw down, dug up and burned with fire. Their spoil, their goods, their riches without number
44. I carried away. A great image of my majesty I made; I inscribed upon it the glory of ASSUR the great lord, my lord, and the power of my empire; I set (it) up (in) the city of SALURIA *at the* ?*foot* (?) of QIRÊQI.
45. From the country of ENZITE I departed; the river ARSANIA[3] I crossed. To the country of SUKHME I approached. UASHTAL its stronghold I captured. The [land] of SUKHME throughout its extent
46. I overthrew, dug up (and) burned with fire. Sua their governor with my hand I captured. From the country of SUKHME I departed; into the country of DAYAENI[4] I descended. The city of DAYAENI
47. with all its territory I conquered. Their cities I threw down, dug up (and) burned with fire. Their spoil, their goods (and) abundant wealth I took. From the country of DAYAENI I departed;
48. to ARZASKU[5] the royal city of Arrame of ARARAT I approached. Arramu of ARARAT before the splendour of my powerful weapons
49. and my violent onset trembled and abandoned his city; to the mountains of ADDURI he ascended.

---

[1] [For Enzite, the Anzitênê of classical geography, see *Records of the Past*, new series, i. p. 103, note 2.—ED.]
[2] [Or "belonging to the country of Isua." See the inscription of Tiglath-pileser I, Column III, line 91.—ED.]
[3] The Arsanias of classical geography, now called the Murad-Su.
[4] [The Diyaveni or kingdom of the son "of Diaus" of the Vannic texts, which lay upon the Murad-Su in the neighbourhood of Melasgerd. One of its cities, Quais, is now represented by Yazlu-tash.—ED.]
[5] [Also called Arzaskun. The destruction of Arzasku and the defeat of Arrame seem to have led to the overthrow of his dynasty. Immediately afterwards Sarduris I, the son of Lutipris, built the citadel of Van, and founded a new kingdom on the shores of Lake Van.—ED.]

After him I ascended the mountains. A hard battle in the mountains I fought; 3400
50. of his soldiers I slew with weapons. Like HADAD [1] I poured a deluge upon them. (With) their blood I dyed (the mountains) like wool. His camp I took from him;
51. his chariots, his *litters* (?), his horses, his colts, (his) calves, his riches, his spoil, (and) his abundant goods I brought back from the mountains. ARRAMU, to save
52. his life ascended the inaccessible mountains. In the energy of my manhood I trampled on his country like a wild bull; I reduced his cities to ruins. ARZASKU together with the towns
53. which (were) dependent on it I threw down, dug up (and) burned with fire. I erected pyramids of heads at the entrance of his great gate. [Some of the survivors] alive within
54. [the pyramids I immured]; others I impaled on stakes round about the pyramids. From ARZASKU I departed; to the mountains
55. [of ERITIA I ascended]. A great image of my majesty I made. The glory of ASSUR my lord and the mighty deeds of my empire which I had wrought in the land of ARARAT upon it
56. [I inscribed. On the mountains of ERI]TIA I set (it) up. From mount ERITIA I departed; the city of ARAMALE [2] I approached. Its towns I threw down, dug up (and) burned with fire.
57. From ARAMALE I departed; to the city of ZANZIUNA [I approached], . . . he trembled; he took my feet.
58. Horses trained to the yoke, oxen (and) sheep I received from him. I granted pardon to [him] . . . [On] my [return?], to the sea

---

[1] Or Rimmon.

[2] [*Aramalis* would be a Vannic adjective, formed by a suffix *li*, and signifying "belonging to Arama." It had evidently been built by King Aramas or Aramis.—ED.]

59. of the country of NAIRI[1] I descended; I purified the forceful weapons of ASSUR in the sea. [I sacrificed] victims. [An image of my majesty] I made; the glory

60. of ASSUR the great lord, my lord, the exploits of my valour and the deeds of my renown I inscribed upon it. [From the sea] I departed; to the country of GUZAN

61. I approached. Asâu the king of the country of GUZAN with his brothers (and) his sons came forth to meet me [and took the feet] of my majesty. Horses

62. trained to the yoke, oxen, sheep, wine (and) 7 camels with two humps I received from him. A great image of my majesty I made. The glory of ASSUR the great lord, my lord,

63. and the illustrious deeds of my empire which I had wrought in the land of NAIRI I inscribed upon it; in the middle of his city, in his temple, I set (it) up. From the country of GUZAN I departed;

64. to SHILAYA the stronghold of Kâki the king of the city of KHUPUSHKIA I approached. The city I besieged, I captured. Their numerous fighting men I slew; 3000 of them as prisoners, their oxen,

65. their sheep, horses, colts, (and) calves to a countless number I carried away; to my city of ASSUR I brought (them). The defiles of the country of ENZITE I entered; by the defiles of the country of KIRRURI

66. which commands[2] the city of ARBELA I came out.— As for Akhuni the son of Adini, who with the permission of the kings my fathers had acquired power and strength, in the beginning of my reign, in the eponymy

67. of the year called after my own name I departed from NINEVEH, TIL-BARSIP his stronghold I besieged, I

---

[1] Lake Van.   [2] Literally "at the head of."

surrounded him with my soldiers, I fought a battle in the midst of it,
68. I cut down his plantations, I rained upon him arrows (and) javelins, before the splendour of my weapons (and) the glory of ASSUR he trembled and abandoned his city,
69. to save his life he crossed the EUPHRATES,—(again) in the second year in the eponymy of Assur-bunâya-utsur [1] I pursued after him; SHITAMRAT, a mountain peak on the bank of the EUPHRATES,
70. which hangs from the sky like a cloud, he made his stronghold. By the command of Assur the great lord, my lord, and NERGAL who marches before me, I approached the mountain of SHITAMRAT,
71. within which none of the kings my fathers had penetrated. In three days a soldier scaled the mountain, a hero whose heart led (him) to the fray, (who) climbed up on his feet. The mountain
72. I stormed. Akhuni trusted to the multitude of his troops and came forth to meet me; he drew up (his) array. I launched among them the weapons of ASSUR my lord; I utterly
73. defeated them. I cut off the heads of his soldiers and dyed the mountains with the blood of his fighting-men. Many of his (people) flung themselves against the rocks of the mountains. A hard battle in the midst of his city
74. I fought. The terror of the glory of ASSUR my lord overwhelmed them; they descended (and) took my feet. Akhuni with his troops, chariots, his *litters* (?) and the many riches of his palace,
75. whose weight could not be estimated, I caused to be brought before me; I transported (them) across the TIGRIS; I carried (them) to my city of ASSUR. As men of my own country I counted the inhabitants. —In this same year I marched against the country of MAZAMUA.[2] Into the defiles

---

[1] B.C. 856.
[2] See *Records of the Past*, new series, p. 149, note 6.

76. of the country of BUNAIS (?)[1] I entered: the cities of Nikdime (and) Nigdera[2] I approached. They trembled before the splendour of my powerful weapons and violent onset, and
77. took refuge on the sea[3] in coracles of willow. In boats of seal-skin I followed after them. A hard battle I fought in the middle of the sea (and) utterly defeated them.
78. The sea with their blood I dyed like wool.—In the eponymy of Dayan-Assur,[4] on the 14th day of the month Iyyar, I departed from NINEVEH; the TIGRIS I crossed; to the cities
79. of Giammu on the river BALIKH I approached. (Before) the fear of my lordship (and) the splendour of my forceful weapons they trembled and with their own weapons Giammu their lord
80. they slew. Into the cities of KITLALA[5] and TIL-SA-TURAKHI[6] I entered. I introduced my gods into his palaces; I made a feast in his palaces.
81. I opened (his) treasury; I saw his stored-up wealth; his riches (and) his goods I carried away; to my city of ASSUR I brought (them). From KITLALA I departed; to the city of KAR-SHALMANESER
82. I approached. In boats of seal-skin for the second time I crossed the EUPHRATES at its flood. The tribute of the kings of the farther[7] bank of the EUPHRATES, of Sangar
83. of the city of CARCHEMISH, of Kundashpi of the city of KUMMUKH,[8] of Arame the son of Gusi, of Lalli of the city of MELID,[9] of Khayanu the son of Gabaru,

---

[1] [The reading of the last syllable is doubtful; we should perhaps read Bunae. See my "Memoir on the Vannic Inscriptions," *Jrl. R.A.S.*, xiv. 3, p. 396.—ED.]

[2] Called Nigdiara on the Black Obelisk, line 51.   [3] Lake Van.

[4] [B.C. 854. According to the Black Obelisk (ll. 54 *sq.*), however, the events here recorded took place two years later in B.C. 852, during the eponymy of Samas-bela-utsur.—ED.]

[5] Or Lillala.   [6] Or Til-sa-Balakhi, "The mound of the Balikh."
[7] That is, western.   [8] Komagene.
[9] The modern Malatiyeh.

84. of Girparuda of the country of the PATINIANS, (and) of Girparuda of the country of the GAMGUMIANS, silver, gold, lead, copper (and) vases of copper
85. in the city of ASSUR-UTIR-ATSBAT on the farther side of the EUPHRATES, which (is) upon the river SAGURI, which the HITTITES
86. call PITRU, I received. From the banks of the EUPHRATES I departed; to the city of KHALMAN[1] I approached. They were afraid to fight (and) took my feet.
87. Silver (and) gold as their tribute I received. I offered sacrifices before DADDA[2] the god of KHALMAN. From KHALMAN I departed. To the cities
88. of Irkhulêni the HAMATHITE I approached. The cities of ADENNU,[3] MASHGÂ[4] (and) ARGANA his royal city I captured. His spoil, his goods,
89. (and) the riches of his palaces I removed; his palaces I delivered to the flames. From the city of ARGANA I departed; to the city of QARQARA I approached.
90. QARQARA his royal city I threw down, dug up (and) burned with fire; 1200 chariots, 1200 *litters* (?) (and) 20,000 men from Dadda-idri
91. of the [country] of DAMASCUS, 700 chariots, 700 *litters* (?) (and) 10,000 men from Irkhulêni the HAMATHITE, 2000 chariots (and) 10,000 men from Ahab
92. the ISRAELITE;[5] 500 men from the GUANS;[6] 1000 men from the EGYPTIANS; 10 chariots (and) 10,000 men from the IRQANATIANS;[7]

---

[1] [Or Khalvan, Aleppo. Compare Helam in 2 Sam. x, 17.—ED.]
[2] [According to K 2100. i. 7, 16, 17, Addu and Dadu were the names given to Rimmon in Syria, Adad or Hadad being a further name by which the god was known in Assyria. Besides Dadu we also find the forms Dadda and Dadi. In Hadad-Rimmon (Zech. xii. 11) the two names of the Air-god are united, while a comparison of 2 Sam. viii. 10 with 1 Chr. xviii. 9 (Jo-ram and Hado-ram) shows that at Hamath Hado or Addu was identified with the national god of Israel. In the Babylonian contract-tablets the name of the Syrian god Ben-Hadad appears as Bin-Addu.—ED.]
[3] [Probably the Eden of Amos i. 5.—ED.]   [4] Or Bargâ.
[5] *Akhabbu mat 'Sir'alâ*.   [6] Probably the same as the Que.
[7] [The "Arkite" of Gen. x. 17. The city is called Irqatu in the tablets of Tel el-Amarna.—ED.]

93. 200 men from Matinu-ba'al the ARVADITE; 200 men from the USANATIANS;[1] 30 chariots (and) 10,000 men
94. from Adunu-ba'al the SHIANIAN;[2] 1000 camels from Gindibu'i the ARABIAN;[3] (and)... 00 men
95. from Ba'asha, the son of Rukhubi[4] of the country of AMMON[5]—these 12 kings[6] he took to his assistance; to [offer]
96. battle and combat they came against me. With the mighty forces which ASSUR the lord has given (me), with the powerful weapons which NERGAL who goes before me
97. has granted (me), I fought with them; from the city of QARQARA to the city of KIRZAU I utterly defeated them; 14,000
98. of their fighting-men I slew with weapons. Like HADAD I rained a deluge upon them (and) *exterminated* (?) them.
99. I filled the face of the plain with their wide-spread troops, with (my) weapons I covered with their blood the whole district;
100. (the soil)· ceased to give food to its inhabitants; in the broad fields was no room for their graves; with (the bodies of) their men
101. as with a bridge I bound together (the banks of) the ORONTES. In this battle their chariots, their *litters* (?)
102. (and) their horses bound to the yoke I took from them.

[1] [Us'û is referred to, the Ushâ of the Talmud, which, as Delitzsch has shown, was not far from Acre.—ED.]
[2] [The printed text has *Si-za-na-â* in mistake for *Si-a-na-a*. Probably "the Sinite" of Gen. x. 17 is meant.—ED.]
[3] *Arbâ*. [4] Baasha the son of Rehob. [5] *Amanâ*.
[6] Only eleven are mentioned. It seems probable that the scribe has omitted the name of one of the confederates.

THE INSCRIPTION OF SHALMANESER II ON THE GATES OF BALAWÂT

TRANSLATED BY THE REV. V. SCHEIL

IN 1877 Mr. Hormuzd Rassam discovered the remains of some very interesting Assyrian buildings in a small mound called Balawât, about fifteen miles to the east of Mosul and nine miles from the mounds of Nimrûd. They consisted of the enclosure of a palace, within which was a chapel dedicated to Makhir, the god of dreams. The temple had been built and the palace restored by Assur-natsir-pal, who named the place Imgur-Bel. The palace was further embellished by Shalmaneser II, the son of Assur-natsir-pal. He furnished it with two folding gates of great size, each of which was ornamented with seven horizontal bands of bronze. The bronze bands not only ran across the faces of the wooden gates, but also round one side of the bronze posts to which the gates were attached. The bands are covered with *repoussé* work, representing the various countries and cities conquered by Shalmaneser in the course of his campaigns. Each band contains two lines of such representations; over each of the pictures is an explanatory inscription, and on either side of the band is a border of rosettes. The bronze plates were fastened to the gates by nails driven through the centre of the rosettes.

The inscriptions, so far as they are still legible, have been published and translated by Mr. Pinches in the *Transactions of the Society of Biblical Archæology*, vii. 1 (1880), and in *The Bronze Ornaments of the Palace Gates of Balawât* (1880-81). The translation which follows will be found to represent the progress that has been made in Assyrian decipherment since the publication of Mr. Pinches.

THE INSCRIPTION OF SHALMANESER II ON THE GATES OF BALAWÂT

COLUMN I

1. Shalmaneser, the great king, the powerful king, the king of hosts, [the king of Assyria] . . .
2. the pitiless one, who subjugates the rebellious . . . [who a rival]
3. has not. The great, the incomparable, the heroic one, . . . [clothed]
4. with splendour, who fears not opposition; [who from the rising of the sun]
5. to the setting of the sun commands . . .
6. is powerful. In those days, through the great lord, Merodach . . . . . .

COLUMN II

1. . . . [After that the gods] had placed in my hands the insignia of mankind, with the help of Assur, the great lord, my lord, and of the god who loves my priesthood, [I trod] the summits of all mountain-ranges
2. to the extremities of them all, [as far as] the sea of Nairi and the sea of Zamua-sa-Bittani [1] and the great sea of Syria. The country of the Hittites, to its very extremities, like a mound
3. swept by the wind, I ravaged . . . I spread over the country of the Hittites the [terror] of the glory of my sovereignty. In my passage from the sea [2] I

---

[1] See *Records of the Past*, new series, p. 149, note 6.
[2] Lake Van.

erected a great image of my majesty, (and) set (it) up along with that of Assur-irbe.¹

4. . . . I marched [to] the great [sea]; I purified my weapons in the waters; I offered sacrifices to my gods; I received the tribute of all the kings of the shores of the sea.

5. . . . I erected [an image of my majesty beside] the sea; I wrote upon it; I set it up overlooking the sea. From the country of ENZITE to the country of DAYAENI, from the country of DAYAENI to

6. [the country of] . . . I possessed myself [of ARZASH-KUN, the royal city of Ara]me, of the land of ARARAT, I threw (it) down, dug (it) up and burnt (it) with fire. While I was staying in ARZASHKUN, Arame, of the country of ARARAT, to the multitude of his forces

COLUMN III

1. trusted and gathered all his troops; to give combat and battle he came against me. I utterly defeated him; I cut his fighting-men to pieces. I slew with weapons 3000 of his soldiers. With the bodies of his warriors

2. I filled the broad plain; I took from him his engines of war, his royal treasures (and) numerous war-material. To save his life he ascended an inaccessible mountain. Like HADAD² I overthrew the widespread land of QUTE.³ From the city of ARZASHKUN to the country of GUZAN,

3. from the country of GUZAN to the country of KHUPUSH-KIA, like the stormy Air-god I roared upon them. I displayed over the country of ARARAT the splendour of my sovereignty. Akhuni the son of Adini,

¹ See Monolith Inscription, II. 10 (above, p. 61).
² [Rather Nerra the demon of pestilence. See my Lectures on the *Religion of the Babylonians*, pp. 195, 311-314.—ED.]
³ [Also called Gutium. It was the district which lay to the east of Assyria, and in early Chaldean geography included Assyria itself. Here, however, the term is extended so as to include not only Kurdistan, but also the district between Assyria and Lake Van.—ED.]

who, with the permission of the kings my fathers, power and strength

4. had acquired, (whom) at the beginning of my reign I had shut up in his city, whose crops I had gathered, whose plantations I had cut down, to save (his) life had crossed the EUPHRATES (and) the city of SHI-TAMRAT, a mountain-peak which hangs from the sky like a cloud, for

5. his stronghold had taken. For the second time[1] I pursued after him; the mountain-peak I besieged. My soldiers swooped upon them like birds of prey.[2] I captured 17,500 of his troops. Akhuni with his troops, his gods, his chariots

6. (and) his horses, I caused to be brought before me; I carried (them) to my city of ASSUR [and settled them among the people of my own land.]

COLUMN IV

1. In the eponymy of Samas-bel-utsur,[3] in the time of Merodach-sum-iddin the king of BABYLONIA,[4] Merodach-bel-usâte his brother revolted against him. They divided the country into (two) factions. Merodach-sum-iddin to ask help to Shalmaneser sent

2. his ambassador. Shalmaneser, the impetuous chief, whose trust is ADAR,[5] took the road; he gave the order to march against AKKAD.[6] I approached the city of ZABAN;[7] victims before HADAD[8] my lord

3. I sacrificed. I departed from ZABAN; to the city of MÊ-TURNAT I approached;[9] the city I besieged, I captured; his fighting-men I slew; his spoil I

---

[1] Literally, "year."
[2] [More exactly "Vultures." The *su* or "Vulture" was the symbol of the god of "the storm-cloud" who was believed to have stolen the laws and attributes of Bel for the benefit of mankind, and to have been punished for the theft by transformation into a vulture. See my Lectures on the *Religion of the Babylonians*, pp. 293-299.—ED.]
[3] B.C. 852.   [4] Kar-Dunias.   [5] Uras.
[6] Northern Babylonia.   [7] On the southern bank of the Lower Zab.
[8] Rimmon.
[9] "The waters of the Turnat" or Tornadotos, the modern Diyaleh.

carried away. From the city of Mê-Turnat I departed; to the city of Gannanate [1]

4. I approached. Merodach-bel-usâte, the lame king, ignorant how to conduct himself, came forth against me to offer combat and battle. I utterly defeated him; his fighting-men I slew; in his city I shut him up. His crops

5. I gathered in; his plantations I cut; his river I dammed up. In a second expedition, in the eponymy of Bel-bunâya,[2] on the 20th day of the month Nisan, I departed from Nineveh. The Upper Zab

6. and the Lower (Zab) I crossed. To the city of Lakhiru I approached. The city I besieged, I captured. Its fighting-men I slew, its spoil I carried away. From the city of Lakhiru

COLUMN V

1. I departed. To the city of Gan[na]nate I approached. Merodach-bel-usâte came forth like a fox from his hole; towards the mountains of Yasubi he set his face. The city of Arman

2. he took for his stronghold. The city of Gannanate I captured; its fighting-men I slew, its spoil I carried away. I ascended the mountains after him. In the city of Arman I shut him up; the city I besieged, I took. His fighting-men

3. I slew, his spoil I carried away. I put Merodach-bel-usâte to death with weapons. Of the miserable soldiers who (were) with him not one did I leave. When Merodach-sum-iddin had conquered his enemies, [and] Shalmaneser

4. the powerful king had fulfilled the desire of his heart, he exalted thee, O great lord Merodach! Shalmaneser the king of Assyria ordered the march to Babylon; he arrived at Kutha,[3] the city of the warrior of the gods [4]

[1] "The garden of Anat." [2] B.C. 851.
[3] Fow Tel Ibrahim. Men from Kutba were brought to Samaria by Sargon, 2 Kings xvii. 24, 30. [4] [Nergal.—Ed.]

5. the exalted ones, (the city) of the Sun-god of the south. At the gate of the temple he prostrated himself humbly, and presented his sacrifice; he made offerings. He entered also into BABYLON, the bond of heaven to earth, the seat of life;[1]
6. he ascended also to Ê-SAGIL, the palace[2] of his gods as many as there are; before BEL and BELTIS he was seen to pass and he directed their path. Their propitiatory sacrifices (and) pure offerings on Ê-SAGIL

COLUMN VI

1. he lavished. He visited all the shrines[3] in Ê-SAGIL and BABYLON : he presented his pure sacrifice. He took also the road to
2. BORSIPPA,[4] the city of the warrior of the [god]s,[5] the *angel* (?) supreme. He entered also into Ê-ZIDA[6] . . . he prostrated himself before the temple of his immutable oracle, and in the presence of NEBO and NANA
3. the gods his lords he directed reverently his path. Strong oxen (and) fat sheep he gave in abundance. He visited all the shrines[3] in BORSIPPA and Ê-ZIDA ; each time
4. he offered *libations* (?). For the men of BABYLON and BORSIPPA, the vassals of the great gods, he made a feast, and gave them food (and) wine ; with embroidered robes he clothed (them) ; with presents
5. he endowed them. After that the great gods had favourably regarded Shalmaneser, the powerful king,

---

[1] [This is a play on the Accadian names of the two cities which constituted the later Babylon, Ka-Dimirra, "the gate of God," sometimes misinterpreted "the gate of the gods," and Din-Tir, which by a false etymology was mistranslated " seat of life."—ED.]

[2] Compare Is. vi. 1, where the heavens are called a "palace" filled by the train of the Lord.   [3] Bit-ili or " Beth-els."

[4] Here written Dur-'Siahha " the fort of 'Siahha."   [5] Nebo.

[6] [Ê-Zida, "the immutable house," was the name of the sanctuary of Nebo at Borsippa, as E-Sagil, "the house of the high head," was that of the sanctuary of Merodach at Babylon. Both names had come down from the pre-Semitic age.—ED.]

the king of Assyria, had directed his face, had granted the *desire* (?) of his heart and strength, (and) had heard his prayers, I departed from Babylon; [to] the country of Chaldæa[1]

6. I descended. To the city of Baqâni, a fortress of Adini the son of Dakuri I approached. The city I besieged, I captured. His numerous soldiers I slew; their rich spoil, their oxen (and) their sheep, I carried away. The city I threw down, dug up (and) burned with fire. From the city of Baqani I departed; the Euphrates hard by it I crossed. The city of Enzudi,

7. the royal city of the aforesaid Adini, I approached. As for Adini the son of Dakuri, the terror of the glory of Merodach the great lord overwhelmed him, and I received from him . . . silver, gold, copper, lead, iron, *muskanna* wood, ivory, (and) elephants' skin. While I was staying [on the shores] of the sea,[2] the tribute of Yakin the king of the maritime country

8. and of Musallim-Merodach the son of Amukkani, silver, gold, lead, copper, [iron], *muskanna* wood, [ivory, and] elephants' skin, I received.

[1] *Kaldi*, in the south of Babylonia. [2] The Persian Gulf.

A VOTIVE INSCRIPTION OF ASSUR-NATSIR-PAL

TRANSLATED BY S. ARTHUR STRONG

THE following inscription is on a tablet of alabaster, which, with a duplicate copy, was found in a marble coffer by Mr. Rassam in the course of his excavations at Balawât in 1878, and is now in the British Museum. It begins with the genealogy of Assur-natsir-pal and a short account of his conquering advance from east to west, from beyond the Tigris to the Mediterranean, which is repeated almost word for word from his great inscription. (Col. ii. lines 125-131. See *Records of the Past*, new series, vol. ii. p. 161.) The king then records how he recaptured and brought once more within the sphere of his dominion a town or fortress, to which he gave the name Imgur-Bel or "Bel's Delight." The position of this place, which was not far east of the ancient Kalah, is now marked by the mound of Balawât. Here he built a temple to Makhir, whom we know only as the god of dreams, but who doubtless possessed other and more important attributes and functions. It was among the ruins of this temple that the coffer containing the tablets was discovered. The inscription closes with the usual appeal to the future king to respect the pious memory of his predecessor, and to restore the building and replace the tablet in the event of their removal or decay. To him who shall thus act the blessing of Assur is promised; while, on the other hand, the curse of Ishtar is invoked upon him who, with the tablet in view, should insult the memory of Assur-natsir-pal. This work of construction and restoration at Imgur-Bel, left unfinished by the great king at his death in 858 B.C., was taken up and completed by his son and successor, a ruler of kindred spirit, Shalmaneser II.

The tablets are in a state of good preservation, and the writing is regular and clear. They are remarkable for the use made throughout by the scribe of vertical lines of division between words or groups of words, thus:—

Assur-natsir-pal | sarru rab-u | sarru dan-nu | sar kissati sar Assur |

Instances of such a use of dividing-lines are extremely rare in Assyrian inscriptions, whereas on the Persian cuneiform monuments the words are invariably separated, but by a wedge placed diagonally.

The lid of the coffer in which this text was found bears a somewhat defaced inscription of the same character, which, however, ends with the words of line 40 of the present translation.

The text has been published (with an introduction, transliteration, and translation) by Mr. Budge in the seventh volume of the *Transactions of the Society of Biblical Archæology*, p. 59, and in the fifth volume of *The Cuneiform Inscriptions of Western Asia*, plates 69 and 70.

A VOTIVE INSCRIPTION OF ASSUR-NATSIR-PAL

1. Assur-natsir-pal, the great king, the mighty king, king of the world, king of ASSYRIA,
2. son of Tukulti-Uras, the great king, the mighty king, king of the world, king of ASSYRIA, son of Rimmon-nirari,
3. the great king, the mighty king, king of the world, king of the same ASSYRIA,
. the warrior chief, who with the help of ASSUR his lord
5. has marched, and among the princes of the four regions[1]
6. his rival has not had; the king who from
7. beyond the TIGRIS to LEBANON and the great sea,
8. LAQI throughout its circuit,
9. 'SUKHI[2] as far as the city of RAPIQU to his feet
10. subdued; from the source[3]
11. of the 'SUPNAT[4] to the passes of
12. KIRRURI, to GILZANI,[5]
13. from the other side of the lower ZAB
14. to the city of TIL-BARI, which (is) above
15. ZABAN, from the city of TIL-SABTANI
16. to the city of TIL-SA-ZABDANI,

[1] The translator in the *Transactions of the Society of Biblical Archæology*, p. 71, reads *ina malki sar sa kiprat arbata*, having evidently mistaken the wedges of the plural-sign for the character for "king."
[2] The Shuhites of the Old Testament (Job ii. 11), on the west bank of the Euphrates between the Balikh and the Khabour.
[3] *Ris ini*, the source: not *riseni*, as one word, which would be, if anything, an anomalous plural from *risu*.
[4] The Sebbeneh Su, which forms one of the sources of the Tigris north of Diarbekir.
[5] [Or Guzan (Gozan).]

17. the city of KHIRIMU, the city of KHARUTU, the fortresses
18. of KAR-DUNIAS[1] to the territory
19. of my country I restored, and the broad
20. lands of NAIRI throughout its whole extent
21. I conquered. That city I took anew;
22. IMGUR-BEL its name I called;
23. this temple with the brick of my palace
24. verily I built; an image of MAKHIR [2] my lord
25. in the midst verily I set up; to LEBANON
26. verily I went; beams of cedar,
27. of cypress, of juniper I cut;
28. beams of cedar upon this temple
29. I fastened; doors of cedar
30. I made; with a rim of copper I overlaid (them);
31. at its gates I fixed (them); this temple
32. I furnished, I made great; MAKHIR the great lord
33. in the midst I seated; an inscribed tablet in his temple
34. I placed. O later prince of the kings
35. my sons, whom ASSUR shall call,
36. (if) this temple decay, (and) the tablet thou see, and
37. read, its ruins do thou restore; thy name with my name write;[3]
38. to its place do thou bring (it) back! ASSUR the lord, the great one, MAKHIR,
39. who dwells in this temple by their favourite [4] rightly
40. shall triumph; his tablet, his name, his seed in their land may they establish!
41. He who the tablet shall see, and offence in plenty
42. speak, may ISHTAR, lady of fight and battle,

[1] Babylonia.
[2] In *W. A. I.*, ii. 58, 12, Makhir is called "the *daughter* of Samas"; but the same deity is invoked as a male in one of the penitential psalms (*W. A. I.*, iv. 66, 2) translated by Zimmern (*Busspsalmen*, p. 100), and Sayce (*Hibbert Lectures*, p. 355), "May Makhir, god of dreams, rest upon my head!"
[3] There is no need here for an amendment of the text, which is plainly as follows: *sumi-ka itti sumi-ya sudhur*.
[4] The phrase *nisi ini*, literally "the raising of the eyes," means "grace" or "favour," hence the object of such grace or favour, a favourite or darling (*Liebling*, Delitzsch).

43. his weapons break in pieces, his throne
44. take from him![1] He who the tablet shall see, and
45. read, (and) anointing the pavement-stones, sacrificing a lamb,
46. to its place shall restore (it), ASSUR the great lord his prayers
47. shall hear, (and) in the battle of kings, the field
48. of engagement, his heart's desire [2]
49. shall cause him to attain.

[1] By separating *lu* from the verb and giving it a temporal meaning the translator in *T. S. B. A.* (p. 78) has missed the force of this passage, which is clearly precative. See Delitzsch, *Assyrian Grammar*, p. 260.

[2] *Ammar libbi = mâla libbi*, literally "the fulness of the heart;" cp. Esarhaddon, Hexagonal Prism, Col. iv. 41, *amtsu mâla libbi*, "I attained my heart's desire."

INSCRIPTION OF RIMMON-NIRARI III

TRANSLATED BY S. ARTHUR STRONG

THE following inscription is on a pavement slab found at Nimrud, the ancient Calah, and now in the British Museum. It has been published in the first volume of *The Cuneiform Inscriptions of Western Asia*, p. 35, No. 3, as well as (from an incomplete duplicate) by Layard on p. 70 of his volume of *Cuneiform Inscriptions*, and Bonomi in his work on *Nineveh*, p. 339. It has been translated by Sayce in the first volume of the former series of *Records of the Past*, and (into German) by Abel in the first volume of Schrader's *Keilinschriftliche Bibliothek*.

It contains the genealogy of Rimmon-nirari III, whose reign lasted from 811 to 783 B.C., during which time he was ceaselessly occupied in consolidating and extending the conquests of his predecessors. In fact, on the eponym list for this period there is not a single year not marked by a campaign. Among other exploits he subdued Damascus, and forced its king to pay tribute. His empire extended from the borders of Elam on the south-east to the Mediterranean on the west, and included as vassal-states

Tyre, Sidon, Edom, Philistia, and Israel. After his death the Assyrian power of the first epoch, having reached its furthest limits, began to decline.

One of the most striking events of his reign was the revival in Assyria of the worship of Nebo. The latter had not been unknown to the Assyrians, but his cult was not so important with them as with the Babylonians, as is shown by the fact that up to the time of Rimmon-nirari his name rarely enters into the composition of proper names. Rimmon-nirari built a new temple for him at Calah, which, as we learn from the eponym list, he entered in the year 787.

From the concluding words of the inscription on the statue of Nebo in the British Museum (*W. A. I.*, 35, 2) it might even appear as if it had been intended that the worship of Nebo should dominate, or actually supersede, that of all other gods : " Put thy trust in Nebo; trust in no other god! " But if this was the project, it was not successful.

The inscription here translated is remarkable from the fact that Rimmon-nirari, after tracing his descent back to his great-grandfather, Assur-natsir-pal, begins again, as it were, at a point still more remote, and boasts himself the descendant of Tiglath-adar, son of Shalmaneser I., behind whom again there stand the mysterious forms of the otherwise unknown Belkap-kapi and 'Sulili.

But the rendering of the latter part of the inscription is put forward only provisionally, to be contradicted or confirmed by future researches.

GENEALOGY OF RIMMON-NIRARI III

1. The palace of Ramman-nirari, the great king, the mighty king,
2. The universal king,[1] King of ASSYRIA, the king whom, as his child, ASSUR,
3. King of the spirits of heaven (?),[2] appointed, and (with) a kingdom
4. without rival has filled
5. his hand. From the great sea
6. of the rising of the sun to the great
7. sea of the setting of the sun
8. his hand conquered, and has subdued
9. in all entirety. The son of Samsi-Ramman,
10. the great king, the mighty king, the universal king, King of ASSYRIA,
11. the king without rival, the son of Sulman-asarid,[3]
12. the king of the four regions, who upon the land of his foes
13. has laid (his) yoke, and has overpowered (them) like a flood.
14. Grandson of Assur-natsir-pal,[4] the manly warrior,
15. who made wide the dwellings of the troops.
16. Ramman-nirari, the exalted prince, to whom ASSUR, SAMAS,
17. RAMMAN[5] and MERODACH as his helpers
18. have gone, and have extended his country,
19. descendant of Tukulti-Adar (?),[6] King of ASSYRIA,

[1] Literally "king of totality."
[2] *Igigi*, perhaps literally "the strong ones," from *agâgu*.
[3] Shalmaneser II, B.C. 859-824.   [4] B.C. 884-859.
[5] Or Rimmon, the Air-god.   [6] Or Tiglath-Uras, B.C. 890-884.

20. King of SUMIR and ACCAD,
21. descendant of Sulman-asarid, the mighty king,
22. who enlarged E-KHARSAK-KURKURRA,[1]
23. the mountain of the lands; descendant
24. of Bel-kap-kapi, a former king,
25. who went before me, belonging to the ancient time of the kingdom
26. of 'Sulili (?), of which from
27. old time ASSUR has proclaimed the report.

[1] E-kharsak-Kurkurra is here the name of a temple, but it had also, and originally, a cosmical meaning as applied to the world-mountain— that is, to the world conceived as a mountain. And the idea of a world-mountain seems to have passed into that of a mountain in the world, or on the earth, which, as the abode of the gods, recalls the Indian Meru. See Jensen, *Kosmologie der Babylonier*, pp. 201-205.

VOTIVE INSCRIPTIONS

Translated by S. Arthur Strong

I

THE following inscription is on a stone lion found at the entrance of a temple at the foot of the pyramid at Nimrud, and now in the British Museum. It is an invocation to Beltis, the female counterpart or shadow of Bel, and forms an introduction to one of the frequent versions of the standard inscription of Assur-natsir-pal. In line 7 Ishtar, though she appears to be invoked as a separate goddess, is probably to be regarded as an equivalent or personification of Beltis. However, the process by which she assumed the titles, and eventually absorbed the personality of the latter, was a gradual one, and its final stage becomes visible only in inscriptions of the second Assyrian period, particularly in those of Assurbanipal.[1]

The inscription has been published in the second volume of "The Cuneiform Inscriptions of Western Asia," plate 66, No. 1. Lines 7 to 9 have been translated by Zimmern in *Babylonische Busspsalmen,*

[1] See Sayce, *Hibbert Lectures*, p. 273.

p. 22, and notes on two other isolated passages will be found on pp. 197 and 256 of Jensen's *Kosmologie der Babylonier;* but it seems that no complete translation has hitherto been published. The lines as they are given in *W. A. I.,* ii. do not represent the arrangement of the original, but I follow them for convenience of reference.

INVOCATION TO THE GODDESS BELTIS

1. To BELTIS, the great lady, chief of heaven and earth, queen of all the gods, the mighty one
2. of all lands, whose festival is honoured among the ISHTARS, who surpasses in power her offspring, a shining form,
3. who, like the sun her brother, the ends of heaven and earth together enlightens, the strong one of the ANUNNAKI,[1]
4. first-born of ANU, great one of the gods, queen over her enemies, who goes before, troubler of the seas,
5. who tramples the wooded mountains under foot,[2] the mighty one of the IGIGI, lady of fight and battle,[3] without whom in E-sarra the sceptre
6. they would not obey, who causes to receive strength,

---

[1] The spirits of the under world opposed to *Igigi,* the spirits of the upper air.

[2] In an inscription of Assur-natsir-pal on a small altar brought from Balawât by Mr. Rassam, and numbered 71 in the Nimrud Gallery of the British Museum, the same epithet is applied to Bel. *Ana Beli. . . . . mu-na-ri-id khur-sâ-ni a-sib E-kid-mu-ri,* etc.—" To Bel . . . trampling the wooded mountains under foot, dwelling in *E-kid-mu-ri,*" etc.

[3] Or, as Mr. Pinches suggests, "without whom . . . *the herd* or *tribe* would not obey," taking *sibdhu* as a collective expressing literally "that which is driven together." Cf. Ex. xxiv. 4. שִׁבְטֵי יִשְׂרָאֵל "the tribes of Israel." Jensen translates: "*ohne die . . . ein Strafgericht* (?) *nicht günstig ist.*" (1) *E-sarra* is the temple of heaven, opposed to *E-kur,* the temple of the earth.

who causes to find the fulness of the heart[1] of him who loves truth,
7. hearer of prayers, receiver of supplication, who accepts entreaty, ISHTAR, the perfect light,
8. all-powerful, who enlightens heaven and earth, whose name is proclaimed in the regions of all countries,
9. who bestows life, the merciful goddess, to whom it is good to pray, who dwells
10. in CALAH, my lady.

II

In the following inscription Assur-bani-pal commemorates the revolt of Elam and its final suppression (after 648 B.C.), as well as certain repairs or alterations which he carried out in the temple of Ishtar of Nineveh, to whom are gratefully ascribed both the inspiration and the merit of his victorious campaigns.

The reference to the fate of Teumman's successors is not altogether clear, though Tiele (*Babylonisch-Assyrische Geschichte*, ii. 399) is probably right in explaining it as an allusion to the triumphal progress of Assur-bani-pal to the gate of the temple of Ishtar in a chariot drawn by the four conquered kings. See *W. A. I.*, v. 10, 29. But in that case the introduction of Ummanigas must be due to an error, for he was killed by his son, Tammaritu, long before the end of the Elamite war, which this barbaric triumph of Assur-bani-pal was intended to celebrate (Smith, *History of Assurbanipal*, p. 202).

---

[1] Or, "who causes to attain the heart's desire of him," etc.

And, as we learn from *W. A. I.*, v. 10, it was the Arabian King Vaiteh, who, together with the three Elamite princes mentioned in our inscription, was compelled to draw the car of Assur-bani-pal.

The inscription appears to have been frequently copied and widely circulated. Four versions are preserved in the British Museum (Nos. 62, 63, 64, 65), and a fifth was discovered at Tartûs (the ancient Antarados) in 1885, of which the text, with a translation, was communicated by Professor Sayce to the Society of Biblical Archæology, and published in their Proceedings (vii. 142). It has further been published and translated by George Smith (History of Assurbp., p. 303), and S. A. Smith (*Keilschriftexte Asurbanipals*, ii. 10), while a German version by Jensen will be found on p. 264 of the second volume of Schrader's *Keilinschriftliche Bibliothek*.[1]

1. To BELTIS, lady of the lands, who dwells in E-BARBAR,[2]
2. Assur-bani-pal, King of Assyria, the great one, her worshipper,

---

[1] The text will be found in the second volume of *W. A. I.*, plate 66, No. 2; but the arrangement of the present translation is different, being that of No. 64, as edited by S. A. Smith.

[2] It is uncertain whether the name of this temple should be read E-barbar or E-masmas, and the meaning of the name is also obscure. However, in *W. A. I.*, ii. 48, 26, *barbar* (or *masmas*) is explained by the Assyrian phrase *kis-su sa mu-'sa-ri-e*, which is interpreted to mean "library" (Sayce, *Hibbert Lectures*, p. 149), in which case *E-barbar* would be "the temple of the library." The original meaning of *mu'sarû* seems to have been "furrow"; cp. *W. A. I.*, iv. 27, 1: *bi-i-nu sa ina mu-'sa-ri-e me-e lâ is-tu-u* ("seed which in the furrows drinks not water"). Hence, through the idea of what is traced or indented, it comes to mean an inscribed character, an inscription. The temple in question is the temple of Ishtar at Nineveh, which was also restored by Assur-natsir-pal. See *W. A. I.*, iii. 3, 40.

3. the governor, the work of her hands, who by her great command
4. in the onset of battle had cut off
5. the head of Teumman, King of ELAM;
6. and Ummanigas, Tammaritu, Pa'e,
7. Ummanaldas, who after Teumman had exercised
8. royalty over ELAM, with her great help
9. my hands took them, and to the chariot,[1]
10. the car of my kingship I fastened them,
11. and in her mighty name in all countries I went to and fro,
12. and rival had I none. In those days the pavement of the house of ISHTAR,
13. my lady, with squared stone well-hewn [2] its fabric
14. I made great for ever. BELTIS,
15. may this pavement be accepted before thee!
16. On me, Assur-bani-pal, the worshipper of thy great godhead,
17. a life of long days, wholeness of heart bestow,
18. and going to and fro in E-BARBAR may my feet grow old!

III

The following is a translation of the inscription of Assur-natsir-pal referred to in II, note 2. It establishes the identification of Beltis with Ishtar of Nineveh, and also records the fact that "the temple of the library" (?) was originally built or founded by Samsi-Rimmon. Two inscriptions and two only of this ancient king appear to have been preserved;

---

[1] The words translated "chariot" (*itsi sa sa-da-di*) mean literally "the wood of drawing," or "the draught-wood."
[2] *iski*, translated "well-hewn," I take as an adjective, and connect with the root שבה, of which "primaria potestas fortasse est in *secando*." The meaning "strong" has also been suggested; in any case it is difficult to see how it can be made (as by S. A. Smith) into a preterite of the first person.

but in both he styles himself "builder of the house of Assur," which is perhaps the same temple as that which in later records, like the present, we find more particularly associated with Ishtar. The inscription is on a fragment of a votive dish of clay found at Kouyunjik, and now in the British Museum.

1. Assur-natsir-pal, vicar[1] of BEL, high-priest of ASSUR, son of Tukulti-Uras, vicar of BEL, high-priest of ASSUR, son of Rimmon-nirari, vicar of BEL, high-priest of ASSUR,
2. when E-BARBAR, the house of ISHTAR of NINEVEH, my lady, which Samsi-Rimmon, high-priest of ASSUR [2] the great one who went before me, had made,
3. fell into decay, from its foundations to its roof I restored (it), I completed (it), I strengthened (it) more than before, I repaired (it) . . .[3]
4. An inscription I wrote in the midst . . . May some later monarch that which has fallen of it renew; the name written to its place [may he restore !][4]

[1] I venture, on an obvious model, to introduce the phrase, "Vicar ot Bel," as more expressive than such terms as "Viceroy," of the combination of functions in a ruler who was not only a king but also a pope.
[2] The son of Isme-Dagon, cir. B.C. 1820.
[3] At the end of line 3 I restore *u-sa-tir*; cp. *Tiglath-Pileser*, viii. 49, *a-na as-ri-su-nu u-tir.*
[4] I restore *lu-tir*; cp. *W. A. I.*, iii. 3, 23, *ana as-ri-su lu-tir.*

BABYLONIAN CONTRACT-TABLETS WITH HISTORICAL REFERENCES

By Theo. G. Pinches

As it is naturally rare to find contract-tablets with historical references, and as, when such are found, they possess contemporaneous authority on account of their referring to events acknowledged to have taken place, or conditions known to exist, either at or shortly before the date of the document recording them, it is manifest that such documents must be of special interest and unimpeachable trustworthiness. For this reason it has been thought well to collect here a few of the more noteworthy of these important texts—texts which have an additional value in that they do not refer to events touched upon in any known history, though it is possible that references to some of them may be found hereafter.

I.—Rêmut Lends Money to his Needy Neighbours during a Time of Dearth

This inscription, the writing of which is above the average, is divided into four sections. The first gives the text of the transaction; the second the names of the witnesses; the third the name of the scribe, the place, and the date; and the fourth the record of the famine. It is a remarkable text, and possesses a value beyond the mere record, for it shows how great the need of the people must have been. The tablet is numbered 81-11-3, 71.

TRANSLATION

⅚ of a mana of silver from Rêmut, son of . . . , unto Musêzib-Marduk, and Kullâ, his wife, for necessities. In the day when the face of the land sprouts (again), the money, ⅚ of a mana, in its full amount, Musêzib-Marduk and Kullâ shall repay to Rêmut.

Witnesses: Ablâ, son of Arad-bît-Nergal; Sapik-zēri, son of Musêzib-Marduk; Bêl-upakhkhir, son of Tullubu; Ugara, son of Sippê; Nabû-sum-utsur, son of the potter;

and the scribe, Marduk-êdhir. Babylon, month Tebet, day 9th, year 19th, Samas-sum-ukîn king of Babylon.

At this time, in the city of Lami*ma*, want and famine [are] in the land. The people are dying for want of food.[1]

This interesting text is a good proof of the unsettled state of Babylonia at the time it was written.

[1] The following is a transcription of the text:—
Parap mana kaspi sa Rêmut mâr . . . ina êli Musêzib-Marduk, u Kul[lâ], assati-su, ana khubuttu. Ina ûme pan mâti ittaptû, kaspā, parap mana, ina qaqqadi-su, Musêzib-Marduk u Kullâ ana Rêmut inamdinnu.

Mukinnu: Ablā, mâr Arad-bît-Nergal; Sapik-zēri mâr Musêzib-Marduk; Bêl-upakhkhir mâr Tullubu; Ugarâ mâr Sippē; Nabû-sum-utsur mâr pakhari.

U rittu, Marduk-êdhir. Bâbili, arakh Dhebeti, umu tisû, sattu tisû-êsrit, Samas-sum-ukin sar Bâbili.

Ina ume su ina al Lamîma (?) sunqu u dannatu ina mâti [ibassî]. Nêsi ina la makalê imuttu.

VOL. IV   H

It was in the year 648 B.C. Samas-sum-ukîn or Saosduchinos had been on the throne of Babylonia, under the suzerainty of his brother, Assur-bani-apli, for 19 years, and the end of his rule, and his own tragic death, were nearing. The Assyrian army, sent by his brother, was probably at that time overrunning the land, and destroying everything wherever they passed. Hence were the people overtaken by want and misery, such as often happened to them in those days. If we want to know how the Babylonians behaved towards each other during this trying time, the tablet here translated depicts it to us clearly, and it is a picture worthy of consideration. Rêmut, a man probably richer and more fortunate than his neighbours, lends a sum of money which was hardly to be considered small ($\frac{5}{6}$ths of a mana = 50 shekels) to Musêzib-Marduk and Kullâ, his wife, without interest (for none is mentioned). This money is lent, not for a week or a month, but *until the land brings forth again*,[1] whenever that might be. All honour to Rêmut. It is to be hoped that he and his friends passed happily through this trying time when there was " want and famine in the land, and the people were dying for want of food " ; and well has Marduk-êdhir, the scribe, done in recording the fact.

The name of the city mentioned in the last paragraph (Lamîma) is doubtful. The last syllable may be *ra*, in which case we must read Lamira. There

[1] Such is evidently the meaning of the words "In the day when the face of the land sprouts" (ittaptû). *Zêrû taptû* (82-3-23, 775) is apparently "sprouting seed."

is yet a third possibility, namely, that the characters are quite correctly read, but that the final *ma* is the well-known enclitic particle. If this be the case, we must read " At this time, in the city of Lamî also, there is want and famine in the land." After the word *makalê* there is a small piece of the tablet broken away, but this seems to have contained no word of importance, if, indeed, it was inscribed at all.

II.—A Testimony to Babylonian Overlordship in Tyre

The Governor of Kadesh makes a Pledge with Regard to Some Cattle

This little text, which is an ordinary contract-tablet of unbaked clay, is important not only as giving the date of the Babylonian dominion so far from Babylonia, but also for the names, some of which are clearly Phœnician. The text is slightly damaged, but the wanting characters can, in every case, be restored with perfect certainty. The number is 81-4-28, 88.

Translation

On the 15th day of the month Iyyar, Milki-idiri, Governor of Kidis, will get *three* cows and their young, and will give them to Ablâ, son of Nadin-âkhi, descendant of the priest of the Sungod. If he cannot get (them), Milki-idiri will give to Ablâ, son of Nadin-âkhi, son of the priest of the Sungod, 5 mana of silver.

Witnessing: Bunduti, son of Nabû-ukîn, descendant of Nabutu; Musêzib-Marduk, son of Ablâ, descendant of the fisherman (?); Marduk-sakin-sumi, son of Marduk-êdhir, descendant of Êdheru; and the scribe, Pir'u, son of Sulâ. Tyre, month Tammuz, day 22d, year 40th, Nebuchadnezzar, King of Babylon.[1]

The cause of Milki-idiri taking the obligation here recorded upon himself it is unfortunately impossible to determine. Judging, however, from the fact that it is cattle that are given, and that only in event of inability to get the animals money was to be substituted, it may be inferred that he entered into the obligation by way of compensating Ablâ for a loss for which he was in some way responsible. The contract gave Milki-idiri nearly ten months in which to discharge the obligation (22d of Tammuz, or June-July, to the 15th of Iyyar, or April-May).

Special interest centres in the name of the principal contracting party, Milki-idiri, Governor of Kidis. His name forms an analogy with that of Ben-Hadad, whose full name was Ben-Hadad-hidri, the meaning of which, as I have elsewhere remarked,[2] was probably "The Son of Hadad (is) my glory."[3] The

---

[1] Transcription of the Babylonian text:
[Ad]i ûmu khamisserit sa arakh Aari, *salsit* littê û mârê-sunu, Milki-idiri, bêl pîkhâti sa al Kidis, ibbakamma ana Ablâ, abli-su sa Nadin-âkhi, abil sangî Samas, inamdin. Kî la itabbakka, khamsit mana kaspi Milki-idiri ana Ablâ, abli-su sa Nadin-âkhi, abil sangî Samas, inamdin.

Mukinnu : Bunduti, abli-su sa Nabû-ukîn, abil Nahutu ; Musêzib-Marduk, abli-su sa Ablâ, abil ba'iri ; Marduk-sakin-sumi, abli-su sa Marduk-êdhir, abil Êdheru ; u rittu, Pir'u, abli-su sa Sulâ. Al Tsurru, ârakh Du'uzi, ûmu êsrâ-sanê, sattu irbaa, Nabû-kudurri-utsur, sar Bâbili.

The word "three" (*salsit*, line 2) is doubtful.

[2] *Proceedings of the Society of Biblical Archæology* for February 1883, pp. 71-74.

[3] See Gesenius's Hebrew Dictionary (Bagster and Sons), under הָדַר. The Assyrian form of the name Ben-hadad is Addu-idri (-'idri), for Bin-Addu-'idri (Ben-Hadad-heder(i) or -hidri). It is difficult to say whether

most likely meaning of Milki-idiri (= Melech-heder(i) or Melek-hidri) is therefore "Molech (is) my glory." As for the name of the place of which he was governor, Kidis[1] (which was probably pronounced Kedes or Kedesh), this is undoubtedly Kedesh (Kadesh), on the lake of Homs, a site of considerable interest, in that it was the scene of a conflict between Ramses II and the Kheta or Hittites, and is supposed to be mentioned in 2 Samuel xxiv. 6, under the name of Takhtim Khodshi, in the neighbourhood of Tyre and Sidon.[2]

All the other personal names in this text are Babylonian, though it is possible that at least some of the people who bore them were not Babylonians.

About the beginning of July, therefore, in the year 564 B.C., Melek-hidri, Governor of Kadesh, visited Tyre for the purpose of attending to his affairs.

III.—NERIGLISSAR GIVES HIS DAUGHTER GIGITUM IN MARRIAGE TO NABÛ-SUM-UKIN, PRIEST OF NEBO, AND DIRECTOR OF E-ZIDA.

This tablet is one of the class of wedding-contracts, and is unfortunately only a fragment. Such as it is,

---

the Greek form *Ader* arises from a simple (and easy) interchange of the letters *d* and *r*, or from the fact that the last element of the name was *heder* (or *hidri*).

[1] As I have elsewhere pointed out, Qoph changes into Kaph in Assyrian before *e* and *i*, hence Kidis (Kedes) for Qidis (Qedes).

[2] See the Rev. H. G. Tomkins's paper in the *Transactions of the Society of Biblical Archæology*, vol. vii. p. 394.

however, it is a welcome addition to our knowledge, and it is greatly to be hoped that a duplicate, completing the text, will some day be found. The Museum number is 81-11-3, 222.

TRANSLATION

Nabû-sum-ukîn, priest of Nebo, director of E-zida, son of Siriktum-Marduk, descendant of Isdē-îlāni-danan, said to Neriglissar, king of Babylon : "Give Gigîtum, thy virgin daughter, to wifehood, and let her be a wife." Neriglissar [said] to Nabû-sum-ukîn, priest of Nebo, director of E-zida

. . . .

About twenty-eight lines are wanting here, the text becoming again legible at the end of the list of witnesses on the reverse :—

    . . . . son of Nabû-sum-lîsir . . . .
    . . . . ri, son of Nabu-sarra-utsur, the judge (? ?)
    Nabû-sum-utsur, the scribe, son of Assur . . .
    Babylon, month Nisan, day 1st, year 1st,
    [Neriglis]sar king of Babylon. Copy of E-zida.[1]

Although this tablet is not by any means perfect, and the text does not, in its present state, communicate to us the conclusion of the matter, it may neverthe-

---

[1] The transcription is as follows :—
Nabû-sum-ukîn, TU-MAL Nabû, satam E-zida, abli-su sa Siriktum-Marduk, abil Isdē-ilāni-danan, ana Nergal-sarra-utsur, sar Bâbili iqbî : Gigî-tum, mârât-ka batultum, ana assutu binamma lû assati sî. Nergal-sarra-utsur, sar Bâbili, ana Nabû-sum-ukîn, TU-MAL Nabû, satam E-zida [iqbî?]:
. . . . mâru sa Nabû-sum-lîsir . . . ; . . . . . . -ri, mâru sa Nabû-sarra-utsur, [daanu].
Nabû-sum-utsur, dupsarru, abil Assur . . . Bâbili, arakh Nisannu, ûmu estin, sattu estin, [Nergal-sarra-]utsur, sar Bâbili. Gabri E-zida.

less be regarded as tolerably certain that Neriglissar did give his daughter Gigîtum in marriage to Nabû-sum-ukîn; for, had it been otherwise, there would have been no need for this document, the importance attached to which may be gathered from the fact that more than one copy was made, the text preserved in the British Museum being that belonging to the temple (E-zida, the Birs-Nimroud) of which Nabû-sum-ukin was high-priest and director.

As will be seen from the translation, Nabû-sum-ukîn does not use any pronoun when making his request known to Neriglissar. He merely says, "Give Gigîtum, thy virgin daughter, to wifehood, and let her be a wife," or "the wife." An examination of texts of a similar class shows that this was the customary formula. The word for "wife" is written with the usual ideogram, and is unaccompanied by any pronoun. A similar text in the Liverpool Museum, however, spells the word out, and gives the same form, *assati*, as is transcribed in the present article. It is possible, therefore, that this terminal *-i* was always understood and read as the possessive pronoun of the first person, even when not written. Other examples of this grammatical usage exist.

The remainder of the tablet was probably taken up with the usual conditions—the penalty on Nabû-sum-ukîn if he should divorce or abandon his wife; the penalty on Gigîtum if she should disown or forsake her husband; directions with regard to the amount and disposal of her dowry, etc. It is here to be noted that Herodotus was probably wrongly informed with regard to the compulsory nature of the public prostitution of unmarried women practised in ancient Babylonia, for the expressions found in these tablets point, sometimes, as in the present case, to a belief, on the part of the bridegroom, in the chastity of the woman chosen by him to be his wife.

Doubtless the priesthood of Babylon were highly elated that one of their number had allied himself by marriage with the royal family of Babylon, for this must have added greatly to their prestige and influence at the time. The date is March-April, the Babylonian New-Year's Day, 560 B.C.

IV.—THE MEDES AND PERSIANS IN BACTRIA.

SAN-ABÛ-DUPPU SELLS HIS BACTRIAN SLAVE-GIRL.

This text, which is rather mutilated, is an ordinary sale-tablet. Its importance, however, will be easily seen, for it is seldom that records of battles and warlike expeditions are to be found on contract-tablets. It is therefore one of the most interesting tablets of its class, and even the names of the witnesses possess a special value. The tablet is composed of three fragments, which were found by me to join some years ago. The number is 82-9-18, 4215 + 4226.

Translation

Sa-Nabû-duppu, son of Nabû-sarra-utsur, with cheerfulness of heart, has sold Nanâ-silim, his Bactrian slave, from the 5th battle of the sipiri against *dursu*, whose right side and hand are inscribed with the name of Dhîbtâ, daughter of Sin-êdhir, for [... mana ... shekels of silver], which is by the 1 shekel piece, coined, not standard, for the price complete, to Issar-Taribi, son of Mur-êpus. [N.], son of Sa-Nabû-duppu, takes the responsibility [of defeasor, claimant], royal-handmaidship, (or) born-daughtership, which (may be) upon Nanâ-silim. [The money, ... mana ... shekels of silver], which is by the 1 shekel piece, coined, not standard, [the price of the slave], Sa-Nabû-duppu, son of Nabû-sarra-utsur, has received [from the hands of] Issar-taribi, son of Mur-êpus.

Witnessing : Tsillâ, son of Akhume- . . ; . . . . . son of Gamaryāwa (Gamariah) ; Sa-pi- [Bel ? son of] . . . . . ; Barikîa (Berechiah), son of . . . . . . ; . . . . . son of Quddâ ; Samas-iriba, [son of] . . . . . . ; Ilāni-bakhâdi, son of . . . . . . ; and the scribe, Marduka, son of Epes-îli. Sippar, month Iyyar, 18th day, 10th year, Darîawush (Darius), king of Babylon and countries.

At the sitting of Dhîbtâ, daughter of Sin-êdhir, wife of Man- . . . -Samas.[1]

[1] The following is a transcription of the text:—
Sa-Nabû-duppu, abli-su sa Nabû-sarra-utsur, ina khud libbi-su Nanâ-silim, gallat-su (âl) Bakhtaru'iti, sa khamilta mikhkhiltum sa sipiri ina mukhkhi dursu, sa imni-su u sitta-su ana sumu sa Dhîbtâ, mârat-su sa Sin-êdhir sadhdhirta ana [.. mana ... siqli kaspi], sa ina estin siqli bitqa nukhutu, sa la ginnu ana simi gam[rutu, ana Is]sar-taribi, abli-su sa Mur-êpus, iddin. But [sikhi, pakirranu], âmat-sarrûtu, mâr[at-banutu] sa ina mukhkhi Nana-si[lim] . . . . . abli-su sa Sa-Nabû-duppu, nasi. [Kaspâ, . . . mana . . siqli kaspi], sa ina estin siqli bitqa, nukhutu, sa la [ginnu, simi amelutti], Sa-Nabû-duppu, abli-su sa Nabû-sarra-utsur, ina qatâ] Issar-taribi, abli-su sa Mur-[êpus], edhir.
Mukin : Tsillâ, abli-su sa Ahume- . . . ; . . . abli-su sa Gamaryāma ; Sa-pi-Bêl (?) . . . . . ; Barikîa, abli-su sa . . . . ; . . ., abli-su sa Kuddâ ; Samas-iriba [abli-su sa] . . . . ; Ilāni-bakhâdi', abli-su-sa . .

Ina asabi sa Dhîbtâ, mârat-su sa Sin-êdhir, assat Man- . . . -Samas. U rittu, Marduka, abil Epes-îli. Sippar, arakh Aari, ûmu [samasserit], sattu esrit, Darîawus, sar Bâbili u mâtâti.

One of the important points concerning this text is that, by the tenth year of Darius, five battles had been fought with a Bactrian tribe; and it is not unlikely that Sa-Nabû-duppu acquired Nanâ-silim (the unfortunate woman had received a Babylonian name, in accordance with the custom of the time) from the daughter of the man who captured her, namely, Sin-êdhir. The remainder of the contract proper is of the usual kind, and refers, like many others, to the taking of a duty or responsibility by one of the contracting parties (in this case the son of the seller), to guarantee the buyer against any claim hereafter on the part of the seller, his kinsfolk, or the king.

In my first rendering I read the name of the slave as Nanā-khusi; and Khupiri (which I regarded as the name of a Bactrian tribe) instead of *sipiri*. Noting, however, that the *khu* in Akhume (see the list of witnesses) was differently formed, it now seems to me better to read these words as *Nanā-silim* and *sipiri*, which readings I have adopted here. The *sipiri* was a Babylonian official attached to the household of the king and princes of the blood. From our text it would seem that this official also conducted military expeditions, at least in Persian times. What is the meaning of the word *dursu*, against which the *sipiri* seems to have gone, is uncertain. There is no determinative prefix or suffix indicating that it is the name either of a person, a place, or a river, though something of the kind might be expected.

Another point of interest is the names. Issar-taribi, the buyer, a well-known tradesman of the time when the tablet was drawn up,[1] bears one of the most interesting. About the first element, Issar, there is some uncertainty, as it sometimes appears as Istar.[2] This name apparently means "The goddess Issar (Istar) has made increase." His father's name, Mur-êpus, means "the windgod has made" or "created," Mur[3] being one of the names of the windgod Rammānu or Addu (Rimmon or Hadad). To many, however, the two witnesses, Gamar-yāwa (Gamar-Jahwa, " Jehovah has perfected " = Gamariah), and Barikîa (" Jah has blessed " = Berechiah), both being probably—indeed, almost certainly,—Jews, will be of even greater interest. Though Jewish names are not uncommon on tablets of this class, it is to be noted that Jews settled at Babylon had no objection to taking Babylonian names, such as were given to Daniel and his companions. The name of the scribe (though he is seemingly a Babylonian, and the name is a common one) is not without interest, for Marduka is apparently for Mardukâa, "the Merodachite" (worshipper of Merodach), the same as Mordecai, the name of a well-known Israelite frequently mentioned in the book of Esther. It must not be supposed, however, in the case of Mor-

---

[1] See the articles by Prof. E. and Dr. V. Revillout in the *Babylonian and Oriental Record*, vol. i. p. 102, ff. ; and vol. ii. p. 57, ff.

[2] I have a faint recollection of having seen the form Assur-taribi, but I could not find this form again when I looked for it afterwards to quote the reference.

[3] Also *Muru* and *Mermer*.

decai, that he was in any way favouring heathenism in accepting such a name as this, for at that time, the word Marduk (Merodach) often meant simply "god." A tablet I have recently copied, in mentioning the various gods, explains them all as Marduk or Merodach; thus Nergal is "Marduk of battle" (qablu), Zagaga is "Marduk of battle" (takhazi), Bel is "Marduk of lordship and dominion (?)," Sin is "Marduk the illuminator of the night," etc. etc.; and it is manifest that the word "god" may be substituted for Marduk with a very acceptable improvement in the sense. This use of Marduk in the sense of *ilu* is probably late.

It has been thought best, in the translation, for the sake of clearness, to place the reference to the locality where the transaction was made at the end. In the original (as will be seen from the transcription), it comes between the list of witnesses and the name of the scribe.

All the above texts were excavated by Mr. Hormuzd Rassam, in 1881 and 1882 at Babylon and Sippara, the latter supposed to be the Sepharvaim of the Bible.

THE DEDICATION OF THREE BABYLON-IANS TO THE SERVICE OF THE SUN-GOD AT SIPPARA

TRANSLATED BY THE EDITOR

THE text of the following curious document has been published by Dr. Strassmaier in his *Inschriften von Cambyses König von Babylon*, Part I, No. 273 (Leipzig, 1890). It has unfortunately been injured in one or two places, though in each case the reading can be restored with more or less probability. The text describes the dedication of three young men by their mother, Ummu-dhabat, to the service of the Sun-god of Sippara, and thus offers an interesting parallel to the history of the dedication of Samuel by his mother Hannah (1 Sam. i.) Samuel, however, was " brought unto the house of the Lord in Shiloh " as soon as he had been weaned, whereas the Babylonian mother waited until her sons were grown up and had been "counted among the men," before she presented them to Samas the Sun-god.

They then became attached to "the house of the males" (*bit zikari*), of which we hear several times in the tablets published by Dr. Strassmaier.

Thus we are told that on the 6th day of the month Iyyar, in the 5th year of Kambyses, a large quantity of dates were conveyed from the *sutummu* or "storehouse" of the king for the support of "the males" and their superintendant Takh-Gula, on account of their ministry in the temple during the preceding month of Nisan; while ten measures of dates were delivered to a certain Arduya for their use in the service of the goddess Anunit during the month of Iyyar.[1] So, again, on the 21st day of the month Ab in the same year, sixty measures of tribute (*makka'su*, Heb. *meke's*, Numb. xxxi. 28) were registered as having been provided for them and their superintendent on account of the "daily sacrifice" during the month Elul.[2] It would therefore seem that a Babylonian temple had attached to it a sort of college of priests, who lived together apart from women, under a head or president, and who were called upon to perform certain religious functions in the services of the temple. It is possible that the priests, who are specially distinguished by the title of "males," were celibates. At all events they could be dedicated to the service of the gods by their mothers, just as Samuel was by Hannah.

The college or "house of the males" reminds us of the Roman *collegia*, as well as of the cells inhabited by the celibate monks who were attached to the Serapeum at Alexandria. It also reminds us of the

---

[1] Strassmaier *l. c.* No. 274. The *sutummu*, over which an officer called the *satam* presided, is the Egyptian *larit*, for which see *Records of the Past*, new series, vol. iii. pp. 7 *sq*.   [2] Strassmaier, No. 281.

account given in the book of Daniel of the education of Daniel and his three companions, though in their case it was a temporary isolation from female society and not a perpetual dedication to divine worship, and was, moreover, intended to fit them for the service of the king and not of the gods.

THE DEDICATION OF THREE BABYLONIANS TO DIVINE SERVICE

THE woman Ummu-dhabat,[1] the daughter of Nebo-bil-utsur, the wife of Samas-yuballidh, the son of Bel-Ê-Babara the priest of SAMAS,[2] who has brought a tablet to him,[3] and also Samas-edhir, Nidittuv, and Arad-Kin,[4] her sons [three in number[5]], (and) who has spoken as follows to Bel-yuballidh, the priest of SIPPARA:[6] "They have not (yet) entered the House of the Males; with my sons I have lived; with my sons I have grown (old) since they were little,[7] until they have been counted among the men"; on the day when Ummu-dhabat [has said this], may she enter the House of the Males, according to[8] the writing of the document which (is) before Bel-yuballidh the priest of SIPPARA for . . . . Samas-edhir, Nidittuv, [and Arad-

---

[1] The name signifies "The mother is good."

[2] The Sun-god, the presiding deity of Sippara, where the great temple of E-Babara, or E-Parra, was dedicated to him.

[3] Among a literary and business-like people like the Babylonians no act was valid unless embodied in writing, and drawn up according to the legal forms. Consequently a mere verbal declaration, as in the case of Hannah, was not sufficient; it had to be accompanied by the prescribed legal document with the names of the witnesses attached to it.

[4] "The servant of Kin." The triad or trinity of deities worshipped at Sippara consisted of Samas, A (who, in the Semitic period, was regarded as the wife of the Sun-god), and Kin (perhaps the son of Samas and A). The reading of the last name is doubtful, and may be Khur.

[5] The traces of the characters given by Dr. Strassmaier show that this must be the reading (*sal-si anna*).

[6] Sippara, written Sippar in the cuneiform, the Sepharvaim or "two Sipparas" of the Old Testament (2 Kings xvii. 31, etc.), is now represented by the mounds of Abu Habba and Anbar (?). It consisted of two cities, one known as "Sippara of Samas," and the other as "Sippara of Anunit."

[7] 'Sikhurrutû.   [8] We must read *aki* instead of *adi*.

THE DEDICATION OF THREE BABYLONIANS 113

Kin] her [three] sons she gives to [the service of the Sun-] god. The witnesses are: Nebo-zira-yukin the son of Bel-[natsir] the son of Mukallim, Bel-natsir the son of Samas-yuballidh; Nebo-[musetiq-udda] the son of Tsillâ; Rimut the son of Musezib-Bel, the son of Babutu; [. . . . the son] of Bel-yukin, the son of Rimmon-yumê: (dated) [SIPPARA¹] the 21st day of the month Nisan, the fifth year òf Kambyses, king of BABYLON, the king of the world.

¹ The characters are illegible here, but the fact that Ummu-dhabat appeared before the priest of Sippara shows that we must supply the name of that city.

THE GREAT INSCRIPTION OF ARGISTIS ON THE ROCK OF VAN

TRANSLATED BY THE EDITOR

THE following inscription is engraved in cuneiform characters, but in the Vannic language, on the face of the cliff on which stands the castle of Van in Armenia. It records the conquests of Argistis, the son and successor of Menuas, who widely extended the empire of Bianias or Van in the early part of the eighth century B.C., at a time when Assyria was in a state of weakness. The Vannic armies marched victoriously in all directions, and even threatened the frontiers of Assyria. As will be seen from the Assyrian Chronicle, of which a translation is given in the *Records of the Past*, new series, ii. p. 123, the reign of Shalmaneser III was mainly spent in war with Ararat or Armenia. His successor, Assur-dân, seems to be referred to by Argistis in this inscription (No. ii. 52).

The inscriptions of which the text is composed are cut below the site of the citadel built by Sarduris I, the founder of the Vannic monarchy (B.C. 840). They begin to the right of a small chamber excavated in the western face of the rock at the commencement of a flight of twenty steps. Above the steps are the three first inscriptions (I, II, and III), which are divided from one another by vertical lines, and should properly be regarded as the three columns of one and the same inscription. Turning a corner at the end of the steps we reach the entrance into a series of five sepulchral chambers. To the left of the entrance are inscriptions IV, V, and VII, while above it is the mutilated inscription VI, and on the right inscription VIII.

The inscriptions were first copied by Prof. F. E. Schulz, and published in the *Journal Asiatique*, 3d series, ix. 52, in 1840. They were again copied by Sir A. H. Layard in 1850, whose variant readings were published by myself in 1882, and also by Dr. L. de Robert in 1876. The copies of the latter, however, are not trustworthy. Squeezes of the inscriptions have further been taken by M. Deyrolles, and are preserved in the Louvre, where they have been examined by M. Stanislas Guyard.

The inscriptions were first deciphered by myself in 1882, and translations published in my Memoir on "The Cuneiform inscriptions of Van" in the *Journal of the Royal Asiatic Society*, xiv. 3, pp. 571-623. Corrections and improvements were subsequently made in the translations by M. Stanislas Guyard, Prof. D. H. Müller, and myself, and were embodied in a paper I contributed to the *Journal of the Royal Asiatic Society*, xx. 1, in 1888. The following version brings them up to the present level of our knowledge of the ancient language of Van. For a description of the latter reference may be made to the *Records of the Past*, new series, i. p. 163.

The great inscription of Argistis is the prototype of the similar historical inscription carved by Darius Hystaspis on the rock of Behistun, and may have suggested the latter to the Persian king. At all events the bilingual inscription of Xerxes, which is engraved on the south side of the cliff of Van, expressly states that it was his father Darius who had originally intended to have it made.

The inscriptions which follow are numbered XXXVII, XXXVIII, XXXIX, XL, XLI, XLII, XLIII, and XLIV in my Memoir on the Vannic texts.

THE GREAT HISTORICAL INSCRIPTION OF ARGISTIS

No. I[1]

1. One says: This [is the record of the conquest] of countries
2. (and) cities [which has been made]. Argistis says:
3. By the command of KHALDIS,[2] the lord, TEISBAS[3] (and) ARDINIS,[4]
4. the company of the great (gods) of (my) people,
5. the same year I collected (my) chariots[5] (and) troops.
6. On approaching the king who is the son of Diaves[6] I overthrew the king the son of Diaves,
7. I conquered (him). The cities of the country of SERIAZIS I burned. The palaces I dug up. On departing
8. out of the city of PUTIS I removed the *princes* (?) of the countries of BIAS (and) KHUSAS (and) the *priests* (?) of the land of TARIUS.[7]

---

[1] No. xxxvii of my Memoir.

[2] Khaldis was the supreme god of Van. Each Vannic state had, moreover, its own local Khaldis, and these local deities were collectively known as "the Khaldises." The other divinities were regarded as the "children of Khaldis."

[3] The Air-god, identified with the Assyrian Rimmon.

[4] The Sun-god.   [5] Or, perhaps "baggage."

[6] This was in the country which adjoined the western frontier of Biainas or Van, near the modern Melasgerd. It is called Dayaeni, or "belonging to Diaves," in the Assyrian inscriptions. The name of Diaves is also written Diaus. In the time of Menuas "the son of Diaus" was called Udhupursis (Sayce, xxx. 12), and it is probable that it was the same prince who opposed Argistis.

[7] Tarius, which means "powerful," may not be a proper name. In this case we should translate: "the powerful country."

9. On approaching the people of ZABAKHAS I conquered the district of ZABAKHAS.
10. On departing out of the city of UZINABITARNAS, out of the country of 'SIRIMUTARAS, a distant land,
11. the *priests* (?) of the city of MAQALTUS in the land of IGAS I removed. After taking away the lands that belong to the son of Erias,
12. on approaching the country of ABUNIS, I conquered the city of UREYUS, the royal city, together with the inhabitants (namely)
13. 19,255 children, 10,140 men alive, (and) 23,280 women;
14. in all, 52,675 persons[1] partly I slew, partly I took alive.
15. I carried off 1104 horses, 35,016 oxen, (and) 1,001,829 sheep.
16. Argistis says: This (is) the spoil of the cities[2] (which) I obtained for the people of KHALDIS[3] in one year.
17. To the KHALDISES I prayed, to the supreme powers who have given the country of the son of Abiliyanis[4]
18. (and) the country of Ultuzais the relative of Qudhurzas[5] of the country of ANISTIR as a present to the race of Argistis.
19. To KHALDIS, the giver, to the KHALDISES, the supreme, the givers, the children of KHALDIS the mighty,
20. I prayed, (even to the gods) of Argistis the son of Menuas; to the KHALDISES I brought offerings.
21. Argistis says: I have conquered the districts of the country of ETIUS. On departing out of the country of E[TIUS],
22. out of the land of Uduris[6] the ETIUIAN, men and women I carried off. Argi[stis] says:

[1] Literally "5 myriads, 2675 of the men of the year."
[2] Or, "for the city." [3] The inhabitants of the Vannic kingdom.
[4] If the name belongs to the Vannic language it would signify "one who belongs to the place of fire."
[5] The name is written Katarzas by Menuas (Sayce, xxxi. 11) and also by Argistis further on (No. VII. 48) His kingdom had the name of Lusas, and was comprised in the country of Etius. Etius seems to have lain to the north-east of Dayaeni, and to have represented the modern Georgia.
[6] Called Udharus by Menuas (Sayce, xxxi. 2) and also by Argistis further on (No. VII. 52).

23. By the command of KHALDIS the lord, TEISBAS (and) ARDINIS, the company of the great (gods) of the people,
24. the same year,[1] on approaching the country of UMEKU (?) . . .
25. I conquered the countries of URYAS (and) DHAIRTSU[S]; I conquered Muruba . . .
26. I made (his city) a heap of stones.[2] His spoil for a booty I took. Men (and) women [I carried off].
27. I conquered the city of UBARU-GILDUS, the royal [city of Muruba . . .]
28. After [departing] out of the country of KU(?) .. RUPIRAS (and) out of the country of TARRA . . .
29. on [approaching] the city of ID . . KU . . AUS the stones and [spoil I took away];
30. the men and women [I carried off].
31. I conquered the country of IRKI . . .
32. After departing [out of] . . .
33. on approaching the country of ARTARMU . . .
34. the slaves [I] seized[3] . . .
35. the cities . . .
36. [On] departing [out of] . . .
37. out of . . .
38. 3 . . children,
39. 10,000 . . . women,
40. in all, 20,279 men of the year,
41. partly I slew,
42. partly alive
43. I took.

No. II[4]

1. [I carried away] 128(0) [horses, . . .] oxen
2. (and) 1,200,6(00) [sheep. Argistis says:]
3. This [is the spoil of the cities[5] which I obtained] for the people of KHALDIS,

---

[1] We must read *sa-a-li-e*, "year."
[2] This seems to be the meaning of the phrase *gari-ni gar-bi*. That *garbê* (with the plural affix *bê*) signified "stones" we know from the determinative prefixed to it.   [3] '*Su-*[*bi*].
[4] No. XXXVIII of my Memoir.   [5] Or "for the city."

4. which belongs to Argistis . . . the city.
5. To the KHALDISES [I] prayed, [to the powers supreme, who have given] the land of the HITTITES,[1]
6. who have given [the kingdom] of Khite-ruadas [as a present] to the race of Argistis.
7. To KHALDIS, the giver, to the KHALDISES [the supreme, the givers, to the children of KHALDIS the] mighty,
8. Argistis the son of Menuas says : By [the command of KHALDIS] the lord,
9. TEISBAS (and) ARDINIS, the gods [of the country of] BIAINAS,[2]
10. [the company of the] great (gods) of the people, the gods have prospered[3] me.
11. Argistis the son of [Menuas] says :
12. I have brought offerings to the KHALDISES. . . . On approaching the land of the HITTITES
13. I conquered the country of NIRIBA[4]; I overthrew the land of . . URMAS ; all the plunder of it
14. for a spoil I took. The city of . . ADAS, the royal city, I captured
15. for the children of KHALDIS, the mighty ones. On approaching the country of the HITTITES
16. the *priests* (?) of the land of the son of Tualas (and) the *princes* (?) of the city of MALIDHÂ[5] I removed.
17. On departing out of the city of PILAS [I changed its] name. [I crossed ?] the *ford* (?) of the river :
18. I deported the men (and) women of the countries of MARMUAS (and) QA. . . .

---

[1] *Khâte.*
[2] Biainas, also written Bianas, was the native name of the district in which the capital of the Vannic kingdom stood. Through the Byana of Ptolemy the name has passed into the modern Van. Van is now the name of the city which in Vannic times was called Dhuspas, while Tosp, the modern representative of Dhuspas, is now the name of the district.
[3] *Khasi-al-me,* a compound of *khasu,* " conquer," and *al,* " increase," and so meaning " to increase conquest."
[4] The Nirhi or "lowlands" of the Assyrian inscriptions in the neighbourhood of Diarbekir ; see *Records of the Past,* new series, ii. p. 146, note 1.
[5] Melidha is the Melidi of the Assyrian inscriptions, the modern Malatiyeh.

19. The palaces I dug up, the cities I [burned]; 25[2]9 children,
20. 8[8]98 men alive, (and) 10,847 women [I took];
21. in all [22,]274 men of the year, partly I slew, partly alive I took;
22. . . . horses, 17,942 oxen (and) 2 . . . sheep I [carried off],
23. [Argistis the son of] Me[nuas says]: This (is)
24. the spoil [of the cities] which I [obtained] for the people of KHALDIS in one year.
25. [To the KHALDISES I prayed, to the powers] supreme who have given the land of the ETIUIANS,
26. [who have given] the land [of Uduris] as a present to the race of Argistis;
27. [to KHALDIS the giver, to the KHALDISES the supreme], the givers,
28. [to the children of KHALDIS the mighty I prayed, even to the gods of Argistis] the son of Menuas.
29. [To the KHALDISES I brought offerings. Argistis says:]
30. . . . .
31. . . . . . . I carried off
32. [as well as sheep. Argistis the son of Menuas] says:
33. . . . . the gracious [gods]
34. . . . . . . all its [plunder]
35. [for a spoil I carried away.] . . . I destroyed them.
36. . . . . . I destroyed them.
37. . . . . Argistis
38. [the son of Menuas] says: [By the command of KHALDIS, the lord,] TEISBAS (and) ARDINIS,
39. the gods of BIAINAS, the company of the great (gods) [of the people],
40. the gods have prospered (me). The same [year on approaching] the people of UBURDAS
41. I conquered the lands of the inhabitants of UBURDAS the kingdom of Isluburas.
42. [The city] of IRDUAS, the royal city, I captured. The country of UISUSIS I ravaged.
43. I deported the men and women that belonged to them. On approaching the people of KHAKHIAS

44. the palaces I dug up, the cities I burned. The city of BI . . KHAUNIS
45. (and) the inhabitants I burned with fire; [8648] children, 2655 men, alive,
46. (and) 8497 women, [in all] 19,790 persons of the year
47. partly I slew, partly I took [alive]; 232 horses,
48. . . 803 [oxen] (and) 1(?)1,626 sheep [I carried away].
49. [Argistis] says : This (is)
50. the spoil of the cities (which) I have obtained for the people of KHALDIS.
51. To the KHALDISES I prayed, to the powers supreme,
52. who have given the lands of Har'sitas,[1]
53. who have given the armies of ASSYRIA,
54. as a present to the race of Argistis.
55. Argistis
56. the son of Menuas says :
57. The citizens of ASSYRIA

No. III[2]

1. occupied part of the country. I assembled (my) armies.
2. By the command of KHALDIS, the lord, TEISBAS (and) ARDINIS the gods of BIAINAS,
3. the company of the great (gods) of the people, the gods have prospered (me).
4. Argistis [says] : For KHALDIS the giver, for the KHALDISES the supreme, the givers,
5. for the children of KHALDIS, [the great] ones, the possessions of the family of Dadis[3] of the land of KULASIS, a distant country,
6. [I] acquired . . 31,439 children of them . . .
7. . . . I carried off. I carried away (also) the tribes of the country.

---

[1] This seems an attempt to represent the name of the Assyrian king Assurdân.   [2] Sayce, xxxix.

[3] Dadis seems to have derived his name from the god Dadi. As Dadi was the king of Khubuskia in the time of Samas-Rimmon (B.C. 820), it is probable that it is his descendants who are here referred to by Argistis.

8. The same [year, on approaching the cities of MENABSUS (and) DUQAMAIS
9. [I captured the city of . . .] the royal [city]; the country I conquered.
10. . . . . . . of the city of SATIRARAS [1] in the country of BUSTUS.[1]
11. [On approaching] the countries of . . . KHUBILUIS,
12. [BA]RUATAIS and BARSUAIS,[2]
13. I carried away the population of [BARSU]AIS; the cities I burned.
14. [In all,] 5(0)40 men of the year
15. [part]ly [I] slew, partly I took alive.
16. . . . . . . 977 oxen
17. (and) . . . sheep [I carried off].
18. [Argistis says:] This (is)
19. [the] spoil [of the cities] which [I have obtained] for the people of KHALDIS in one year.
20. To the KHALDISES [I prayed], to the mighty powers,
21. who have given the country of ASSYRIA, who have given the countries of . . . (and) BUSTUS,
22. a powerful country,[3] as a present to the race of Argistis.
23. To the children of KHALDIS, the great ones, Argistis says:
24. After restoring the palaces of the country of SURISILIS[4] I settled (in them)
25. the soldiers of ASSYRIA who had occupied part of (my) land.
26. By the command of KHALDIS, the lord, TEISBAS (and) ARDINIS
27. the gods of BIAINAS, the company of the great (gods) of the people,

[1] We learn from the Assyrian monuments that Bustus lay to the west or south-west of Lake Urumiyeh. Satiraras is the Sitivarya of the Black Obelisk inscription of Shalmaneser (line 184).

[2] The Parsuas of the Assyrian texts which was situated on the southwestern shores of Lake Urumiyeh. The Parthians may have derived their name from it. We learn from an inscription of Sarduris II, the son and successor of Argistis, that Baruatais adjoined the country of Babilus.

[3] Or the country of Tarius, a proper name as in i. 8.

[4] Surisilis was the name of a Hittite city according to Menuas; see *Records of the Past*, new series, p. 166, line 5.

28. the gods have prospered me. Argistis the son of Menuas says:
29. For KHALDIS the giver, for the KHALDISES the supreme, the givers,
30. for the children of KHALDIS the great, I collected the AVERASIANS;[1]
31. the country of ASSYRIA I [took] for a possession; I I made [it] part of my country.[2]
32. To DADAS[3] the AVERASIAN I apportioned[4] (it).
33. The same year on approaching the countries of . . .
34. (and) ARKHAVEIS, [the city of . . .], the royal city,
35. (and) 60 (other) cities, (with the) men [and women] I took.
36. On approaching the country of BUSTUS [I conquered the city of ZI]KHARARAS,
37. the city of ABURZIAUS, the city of . . . GIS,
38. (and) the city of QADUQANIUS; the country I conquered.
39. Argistis says: [On approaching the country of . . . . . .] I carried away.
40. On departing out of the land of the MANÂ[5] . . . a distant [land]
41. 18,827 men of the year
42. partly I slew, partly I [took] alive, (as well as) 606 horses,
43. 184 camels, 6257 oxen (and) 33,203 sheep.
44. Argistis the son of Menuas says: This (is)
45. the spoil of the cities (which) I have obtained for the people of KHALDIS in one year.
46. To the KHALDISES I prayed, to the powers supreme,
47. who have given the country of the IYAIANS, who have given the countries of MANÂS[6] (and) BUSTUS

---

[1] The word perhaps means "those who dwell by the water."
[2] This must refer to the Assyrian colonies settled in the north.
[3] Not to be identified with the Dadis of line 5.
[4] *Amû-bi* connected with *ama-ni* "half" or "share," *amas-tu-bi* "I partitioned."
[5] The Mannâ of the Assyrian inscriptions, the Minni of the Old Testament (Jer. li. 27.) They adjoined the eastern frontier of the kingdom of Van.   [6] Or Manâ, also written Manai(s).

48. as a present to the race of Argistis (and) the mighty children of KHALDIS.
49. Argistis says: After I had gathered together the chariots¹ (and) the cavalry,
50. by the command of [KHALDIS] the lord, TEISBAS (and) ARDINIS
51. the gods of [BIAI]NAS, the company of the great (gods)
52. of the people, the gods prospered (me).
53. Argistis the son of Menuas says:
54. For KHALDIS the giver, for the KHALDISES the supreme, the givers,
55. for the children of KHALDIS, the mighty, on approaching
56. the country of the IYAIANS, I conquered the country.
57. The palaces I dug up, the cities I partitioned,
58. The city of ERADHALIS [and the district] belonging to ERADHALIS [I] conquered.
59. Their men [and women I] carried off.
60. The same [year] on approaching the country of the MANAI²
61. [adjoining the land of B]USTUS on the river TURA . . .
62. I made (the cities) heaps of stones; the plunder
63. [for a spoil] I took.
64. Their men I carried away
65. [as well as the] women.

The next six lines are lost.

No. IV³

1. 18,243
2. men of the year
3. partly I slew,
4. partly I took alive,
5. (as well as) 79(0) horses,
6. 100 camels,
7. 22,529 oxen
8. (and) 36,830 sheep.

¹ Or "war-material."   ² Usually written Manâ.   ³ Sayce, XL.

9. Argistis says :
10. For the people of KHALDIS this
11. (is) the cities'
12. spoil (which)
13. I have obtained in one year.
14. To the KHALDISES I prayed,
15. to the powers supreme,
16. who have given the MINNIANS'
17. country,
18. who have given [the country of IRKI]UNIS
19. as a present
20. to the race of Argistis.
21. To the children of KHALDIS
22. the mighty
23. Argistis
24. says : By the command
25. of KHALDIS the lord,
26. of TEISBAS (and) of ARDINIS
27. the gods of BIANAS,
28. the company of the great (gods)
29. of the people, the gods have prospered me.
30. Argistis
31. the son of Menuas says :
32. For KHALDIS the giver,
33. for the KHALDISES, the supreme, the givers,
34. for the children of KHALDIS the mighty, on approaching
35. the land of the MANAI I conquered the country of IRKIUNIS.
36. On departing out of the country of ALGAS which belongs to ASSYRIA
37. 6471 men of the year partly I slew,
38. partly I took alive, (as well as) 286 horses,
39. 2251 oxen (and) 8205 sheep.
40. Argistis says : This (is)
41. the spoil of the cities (which) I have obtained for the people of KHALDIS in one year.
42. To the KHALDISES I prayed, to the powers supreme,
43. who have given the country of the MANÂ,
44. who have given the land of BUSTUS as a present

THE GREAT INSCRIPTION OF ARGISTIS

45. to the race of Argistis the son of Menuas.
46. To the mighty children of [KHAL]DIS Argistis
47. says: By the command of KHALDIS, the lord,
48. TEISBAS (and) ARDINIS, the gods of BIANAS,
49. the company of the great (gods) of the people,
50. the gods have prospered me. Argistis
51. the son of Menuas says: For KHALDIS the giver,
52. for the KHALDISES the supreme, the givers, for the children of KHALDIS
53. the mighty, on approaching the land of BUSTUS,
54. I conquered the country of ASQAYAIS; I destroyed the land of SATIRARAUS.
55. The *priests* (?) of the land of UGISTIS I removed,
56. (and) the *princes* (?) of the land of VUSIS. On departing
57. out of the land of ALADHAIS, a distant country,
58. the country I partitioned; the cities I dug up;
59. their men (and) women I carried off;
60. 1(?)873 men [of the year]
61. partly I slew, partly I took alive,
62. (as well as) . . 80 horses,
63. . . . camels . . . [oxen],
64. (and) . . . sheep.
65. [Argis]tis says: [For the people] of KHALDIS [this is]
66. the spoil of the cities [which I have obtained in one year].
67. To the KHALDISES I prayed, to the powers [supreme],
68. who [have given] the countries of MANÂ [and . . .]DIS
69. to the family of Argistis the son of Menuas.
70. To the children of [KHAL]DIS the mighty,
71. [Argis]tis the son of Menuas says:
72. I restored [the district] (which formed) the satrapy of the son of Argistis,[1]

---

[1] It appears from an inscription of Argistis found at Armavir on the Araxes (Sayce, lxviii) that the district which formed the satrapy of the son of Argistis was "cut off" from the land of Lulus. It was included in the territory of the Mana or Minni, which may, therefore, as Prof. Schrader believes, have extended northwards as far as the Araxes and the neighbourhood of Armavir.

73. (and) I took the hostile land of MANÂ, the kingdom of Hazais.[1]
74. [I seized] the corn-pits (and) *grain* (?)[2] of the country of MANÂ.
75. By [the command] of KHALDIS, the lord, TEISBAS
76. [and ARDINIS], the gods of BIANAS,
77. the company of the great (gods) of the people, the gods have prospered (me).
78. Argistis says. . . .
79. belonging to the cavalry (and) belonging to the whole army . . .
80. . . the corn-pits I approached: I subjugated the country of MANÂ.
81. To the children of KHALDIS, the mighty,

No. V[3]

1. Ar[gistis the son of Menuas says:]
2. By the command [of KHALDIS the lord, TEISBAS and ARDINIS],
3. the gods [of Bianas], the company [of the great gods]
4. [of the people, the gods have prospered me. My armies I collected.]
5. On approaching the country of URMES[4] [I conquered]
6. the land. The population I carried away. On departing [out of the land of . . .]
7. the cities I burned, the men (and) women I took to BI[ANAS].
8. (More than) 14,813[5] of the men of the year partly I slew, partly [I took] alive,

---

[1] Hazais is elsewhere called Hazas (Sayce, lxviii. 1). A later Aza, according to the Assyrian monuments, was the son of Iranzu, king of the Minni in the early part of the reign of Sargon.

[2] *Khailâ-ni*, probably connected with *khai-di-a-ni* and *khai-ti-ni*, "fruit," from *khai*, "to gather in."   [3] Sayce, XLI.

[4] We gather from an inscription of Sarduris II (Sayce, xlix) that Urmes lay to the north-east, beyond Babilus and Baruatais.

[5] One or more wedges are lost at the beginning of the line, so that ten or twenty must be added to the thousands (24,813 or 34,813).

9. (as well as) .. 25 horses, (more than) 1744 oxen (and) 48,825 sheep.
10. Argistis the son of Menuas says: For the people of KHALDIS this
11. (is) the spoil of the cities (which) I have obtained in one year.
12. [To the children of KHALDIS] the mighty, Argistis says
13. thus: Among the people of the king KHALDIS has brought the whole, together with what belongs to KHALDIS
14. (namely) 7(0)66 oxen (and) 50,868 sheep.
15. Arg[istis] says: I laid this tribute on the city.[1]
16. To the children of KHALDIS, the mighty, Argistis says
17. thus: The city of BI[KHURAS] I approached.
18. The city of BIKHURAS in the territory of the country of BAM (with) digging up,
19. removing the rebels of the city out of the sun-light,
20. I caused the country of BAM to be dug up. I verily conquered the city of BIKHURAS.

(*No. VI is destroyed*)

No. VII [2]

1. Argistis [says:]
2. [I] appropriated the whole.
3. I captured the palace. An edict [I issued (?)].
4. The population I carried away; the cities I burned,
5. 3270 men [of the year]
6. partly I slew, partly [I took] alive.
7. I carried off 170 horses, 62 camels,
8. 2411 oxen (and) 614(0) [sheep].
9. Argistis says: For the people of [KHAL]DIS [this is]
10. the spoil of the cities (which) I have obtained in [one] year.
11. To the KHALDISES I prayed, to the powers supreme,

---

[1] That is to say, "I took tithe of the city" for the service of Khaldis.
[2] Sayce, XLIII.

12. who have given portions consisting of the district of DHUARAS
13. out of the land of GURQUS, who have given the MINNIANS'
14. cavalry as a present to the race of Argistis.
15. Argistis says: As the lot of KHALDIS,
16. a sixtieth of the spoil, both a portion of the captives and of the plunder,
17. [from among] the hostile people on the river DAINALATIS I selected.
18. I built the *fortress* (?) of the provinces[1] (of BIAINAS).
19. Argistis the son of Menuas says:
20. By the command of KHALDIS, the lord, TEISBAS,
21. (and) ARDINIS, the gods of BIAINAS,
22. the company of the great (gods) of the people,
23. the gods have prospered me. The cavalry I collected.
24. On approaching the country of MANÂ the population I carried away. The cities I burned.
25. On departing out of the city of the tribe of UIKHIS, in the land of BUSTUS,
26. their men (and) women I carried off;
27. 13,979 men of the year
28. partly I slew, partly I took alive;
29. I carried off 308 horses, (more than) 8000 oxen,
30. (and) 32,538 sheep.
31. Argistis says: For the people of KHALDIS this (is)
32. the spoil of the cities (which) I have obtained in one year,
33. To the KHALDISES I prayed, to the powers supreme,
34. who have given the land of MANÂ, who have given the land of ETIUS,
35. as a present to the race of Argistis.
36. To KHALDIS the giver, to the children of [KHALDIS] the mighty,
37. Argistis the son of Menuas says:
38. On approaching the land of MANAI the population I carried away; the cities I burned.

[1] Suras, literally "the world," which replaces the compound ideograph "countries" in the title "king of countries," or "provinces."

39. The plunder of the city of SIMERI-KHADIRIS, the royal city,
40. for a spoil I acquired. Their men (and) women [I] carried off.
41. Argistis says: I captured in the land of ETIUS
42. the war magazines and *zirbila-ni* of the city of ARDINIS.[1]
43. The same year (my) chariots [2] (and) cavalry I collected.
44. By the command of KHALDIS the lord, TEISBAS (and) ARDINIS,
45. the gods of BIAINAS, the company
46. of the great (gods) of the people, the gods have prospered me.
47. On approaching the land of the ETIUIANS [I] conquered
48. the country of the son of Erias, even the country of Katarzas.[3]
49. On departing out of the land of ISQIGULUS [4]
50. the men (and) women I transported to the country of BIAINAS.
51. Argistis says: To the KHALDISES [I made offerings.]
52. On approaching the country of the son of Udharus [5]
53. the people I carried away; the cities [I burned].
54. . . . . I conquered the city of AMEGU . . .
55. . . belonging to the son of Udharus . . .
56. the plunder . . . . . .
57. a stele I set up . . . . . .
58. the name . . . . . .
59. the royal city of him . . . . .
60. sacrifices . . . . . .
61. . . . . . .
62. .   the name (?) . . . . . .
63. .   . .   .
64. . . . [men of the year]
65. [partly I slew], partly [I took] alive;

[1] As Ardinis was a Vannic word signifying "the Sun" and "the day," it is probable that the language of Van was spoken in Etius, a country now represented by Georgia.   [2] Or "war material."
[3] Called Qudburzas above (No. I. 18).
[4] Isqigulus is shown by another inscription of Argistis (Sayce, xlvii) to have been the district in which Kalinsha is situated, a little to the east of Kars.   [5] Called Uduris above (No. I, 22).

66. 12(00) [horses], 29,504 [oxen]
67. (and) (more than) 60,000 sheep [I] carried off.
68. Argis[tis says:] For the people of KHALDIS this (is)
69. the spoil of the cities (which) [I] have obtained in one year.
70. To the KHALDISES I prayed, to the powers supreme,
71. who have given the land of [TARI]US,[1] a distant country,
72. who have given (it) as a present to the race of Argistis.
73. To KHALDIS [the giver], to the children of KHALDIS the mighty,
74. Argistis says: On approaching the land of TARIUS,
75. the plunder of eleven palaces for a spoil [I acquired].
76. To KHALDIS [I] brought these offerings.
77. Argistis the son of [Menu]as says:
78. For KHALDIS [a sixtieth of the] plunder, both a portion of the captives and [of the spoil, I selected].
79. Many buildings (and) palaces I burned; [I] dug up
80. the *monuments* (?).[2] Their men (and) women [I transported].
81. [I conquered (?)] the country of TAR[IUS] the same [year].

No. VIII [3]

1. Argistis
2. the son of Menuas
3. says: Whoever
4. carries away this tablet,
5. whoever removes (my) name,
6. whoever to the earth
7. brings this,
8. (or) pretends (it is the work) of another person,
9. whoever else
10. pretends: "I have made (it),"
11. whoever the chambers in the rock [4]
12. attached to the inscriptions shall take away,

---

[1] Or "a powerful country."
[2] What is left in the text seems to be part of the ideograph of "tablet."
[3] Sayce, XLIV. [4] Literally "wall."

13. (or) shall flood with water,—
14. as for that person may KHALDIS,
15. TEISBAS (and) ARDINIS, the gods,
16. him with curses
17. four times four, publicly the name
18. of him, the family
19. of him, (and) the city
20. of him, to fire
21. (and) water consign

MONOLITH INSCRIPTION OF ARGISTIS, KING OF VAN

Translated by the Editor

THE following inscription was discovered by Sir A. H. Layard on a stone under the altar of the church of Surk Sahak at Van, and though the beginning and end of it are lost it supplements the great historical inscription of Argistis on the rock of Van, and is therefore given here. It was published by myself for the first time in my Memoir on the "Cuneiform Inscriptions of Van" in the *Journal of the Royal Asiatic Society*, xiv. 4. The translation of it I offered there can now be improved in several particulars. The inscription is numbered XLV in my Memoir.

MONOLITH INSCRIPTION OF ARGISTIS, KING OF VAN

1. On departing [out] of the country of BIAS
2. [I conquered the country of KHU]SAS. On approaching the country of DIDIS
3. (and) the city of ZUAS, the city of ZUAS
4. belonging to the son of Diaus, I partitioned.
5. I set up a tablet in the country of the city of ZUAS.[1]
6. Among the ASQALAIANS 105 palace[s]
7. I dug up; 453 cities [I] partitioned.
8. The people of three countries [I] despoiled.
9. The men with fire [I] burnt.
10. In a part of the country the district of QALIS [I destroyed]
11. (as well as) the city of SASILUS[2] in the country of the ASQALAIANS. [I carried away]
12. 15,181 children, 2734 men,
13. 10(?)604 women, 4426 [horses],
14. 10(?)478 oxen, (and) 73,7(00) [sheep].
15. The [two] kings I reduced to vassalage,[3] (namely) Saski . . .[4]
16. the son of Ardarakis (and) Qabi . . . the son of Baltul.
17. Governors (and) lawgivers I established. The king, the son of Dia(us),

---

[1] This had already been done by his father Menuas, whose inscription has been copied by Schulz and translated by myself (Sayce, xxx).

[2] Sasilus is described by Menuas as "a royal city" of the son of Diaus or Diaves, in the country called Dayaeni by the Assyrians.

[3] Literally "I brought to my side" (*ve-dia-du-bi*).

[4] He is stated by Menuas to be "a native of the city of Khaldiris," a word which signifies "the Khaldirian" in Vannic, and shows that the Vannic language was spoken in the place.

18. I appointed governor. I changed his [name],
19. and he, the son of Diaus, to Argistis
20. brought 41 manehs of gold, 37 manehs [of silver],
21. 1(?)0,000 manehs of bronze, 1000 war magazines, 300 oxen,
22. (and) 2(?)0,000 sheep; and he submitted to (my) laws.
23. In the [land] of the son of Diaus I established as tribute (and) offerings
24. [41 (?)] manehs of gold, 10,000 manehs [of bronze],
25. ... oxen, 100 wild bulls, 300 sheep, (and) 300 war magazines.
26. The cavalry, the horses, (and) the officers [I] took (with me).
27. To the KHALDISES I prayed, to the powers supreme,
28. who have given the land of the ETIUIANS as a present
29. to the family of Argistis; to KHALDIS the giver,
30. to the KHALDISES, the supreme, the givers, to the children of KHALDIS,
31. the propitious, I prayed, even to (the gods) of Argistis
32. the son of Menuas; I brought offerings to the KHALDIS[ES].
33. Argistis says: The whole [of the country]
34. (and) the fortresses of the son of Diaus [I occupied].
35. I conquered the country of LUSAS, the country of Katarzas,
36. the country of the son of Erias, the country of GULUTAKHIKHAS
37. (and) the country of the son of Uidhaerus.
38. I departed out of the country of ABUNIS; the king of LUSAS
39. I reduced to vassalage; as governor of the country of IGAS
40. ... I appointed (him). He submitted to the laws of Argistis.

END OF VOL. IV

www.ingramcontent.com/pod-product-compliance
Lightning Source LLC
Chambersburg PA
CBHW040054100426
42734CB00043B/3260